ADVANCED MILITARY VEHICLE MODELLING

Compendium Modelling Manuals
Volume 4

W0082089

Series Editor: Jerry Scutts

Publication Manager: Rodrigo Hernádez Cabos

Photographs:

Antonio Soler García, Salvador Gómez Mico, Rodrigo Hernández Cabos

Modelling Team:

Javier Sanz Sánchez, Sergio de Usera Mugica, Javier Moreno Rodríguez,
Cristobal Vergara Durán, Joaquín González García

COMPENDIUM

Compendium Modelling Manuals

Advanced Military Vehicle Modelling

This edition published by Compendium Publishing Ltd
1st Floor, 43 Frith Street, London   W1V 5TE

ISBN 1902579 08 9

Printed in Spain

© Accion Press, S.A.
C/Ezequiel Solana, 16, 28017, Madrid, Spain

Publication Manager: Rodrigo Hernádez Cabos
Photographs: Antonio Soler García, Salvador Gómez Mico, Rodrigo Hernández Cabos
Modelling Team: Javier Sanz Sánchez, Sergio de Usera Mugica, Javier Moreno Rodríguez, Cristobal Vergara Durán, Joaquín González García

Compendium Publishing
1st Floor, 43 Frith Street, London, W1V 5TE
Tel: 0171 287 4570

Advanced Military Vehicle Modelling

Introduction

Assuming that the reader has assembled and finished a number of AFV kits, this
book aims to help further the widespread interest in this popular branch of model making.
When building a representative range of international military vehicles it
soon becomes clear that not only does each one differ markedly
in design but that paint finishes and camouflage merit increasingly specialised
techniques if they are to be reproduced accurately. Overall knowledge of what has
become a vast subject is growing in line with the many new publications
covering both AFV design and operations. Just how vast can be readily appreciated
by a visit to almost any model competition.
In this book we examine some tools and techniques that should enable
even the highly experienced to branch out further in the search for time-saving
and easier methods of completing models to a high degree of personal
satisfaction - which is what the hobby is all about.
No particular brands of paint, adhesive or materials have been specified in the book.
This is because the experienced modeller will already have a reliable sources of supply and
the fact that availability of given products varies from country to country.

Jerry Scutts

Compendium Modelling Manuals

A growing library of practical books for modellers

Packed with full colour photographs and clear concise text prepared by experienced professional modellers, these books show how to improve your modelling skills. Whether you are a beginner or an experienced modeller these books will guide you through expert model building tricks and techniques. As the series develops it will include all aspects of the modelling interest and the emphasis will always be on practical advice illustrated by clear, good quality photographs.

64 pages, 195mm x 265mm (10 $\frac{3}{8}$ths x 7 $\frac{5}{8}$ths)
£12.95   USA $17.95

Already Published

Basic Aviation Modelling
Compendium Modelling Manual 1

Advanced Aviation Modelling
Compendium Modelling Manual 2

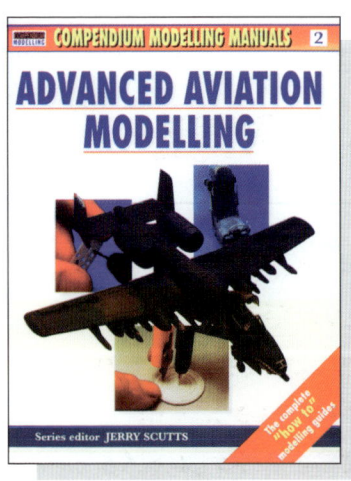
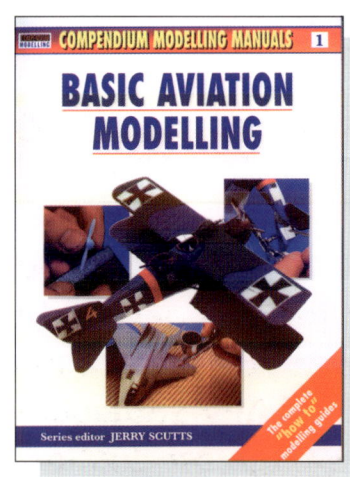

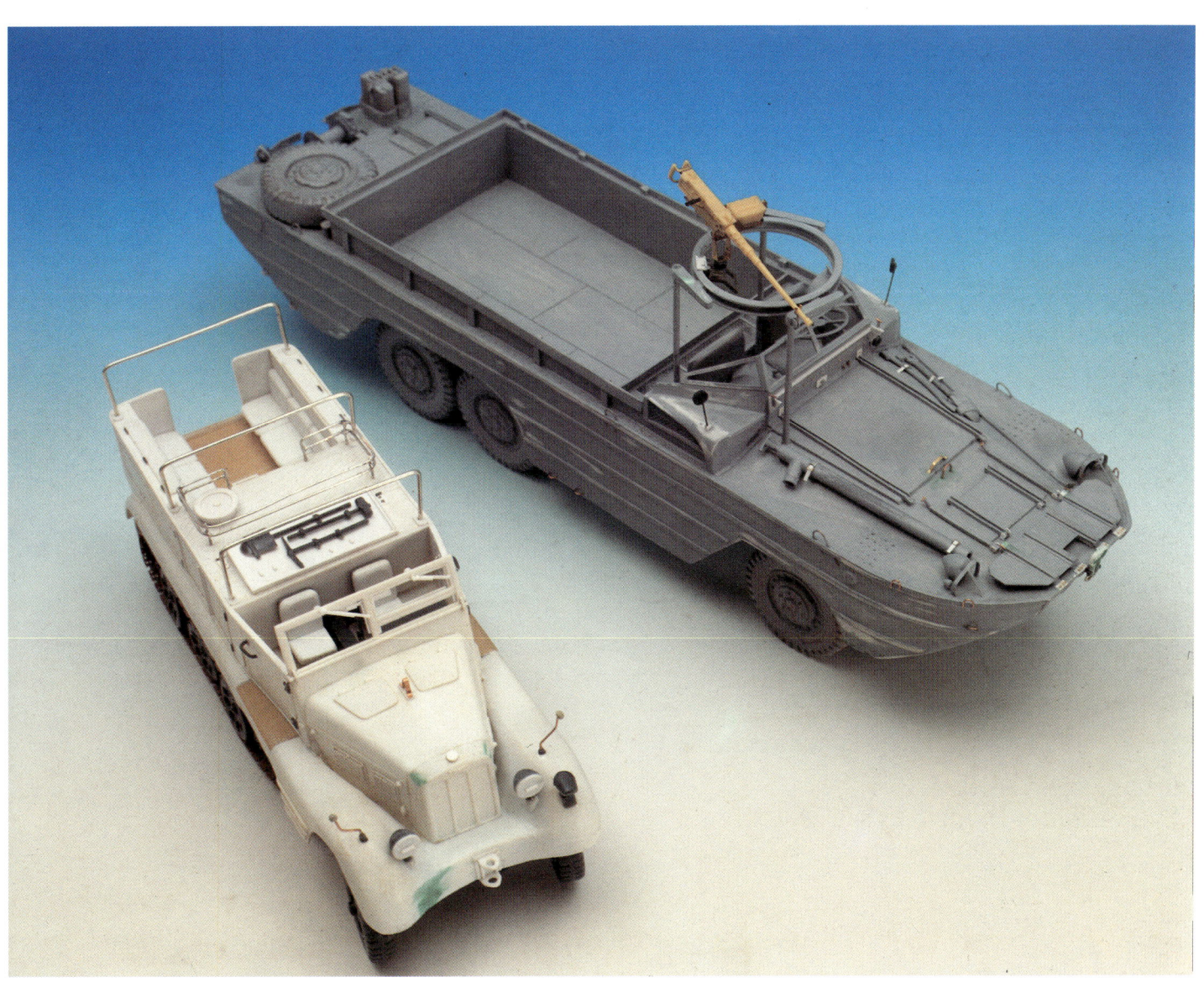

VACUFORMED AND MIXED MEDIA KITS

For some years the vacuforming process offered the modeller the only alternative to injection moulded parts when converting or 'customising' plastic kits. A high standard of detail was possible with vacuforming and a number of AFV subjects were released. The process did not lend itself to huge production runs and those kits shown here have become quite rare. Vacuforms were largely overtaken by highly detailed accessory kits made of resin, modellers opting to combine these - with their excellent durability - with new major component parts cut from plastic sheet. Vacuforms have not entirely disappeared however and still figure in 'mixed media' conversion work on tanks and AFVs.

A VACUFORM MODEL PROJECT

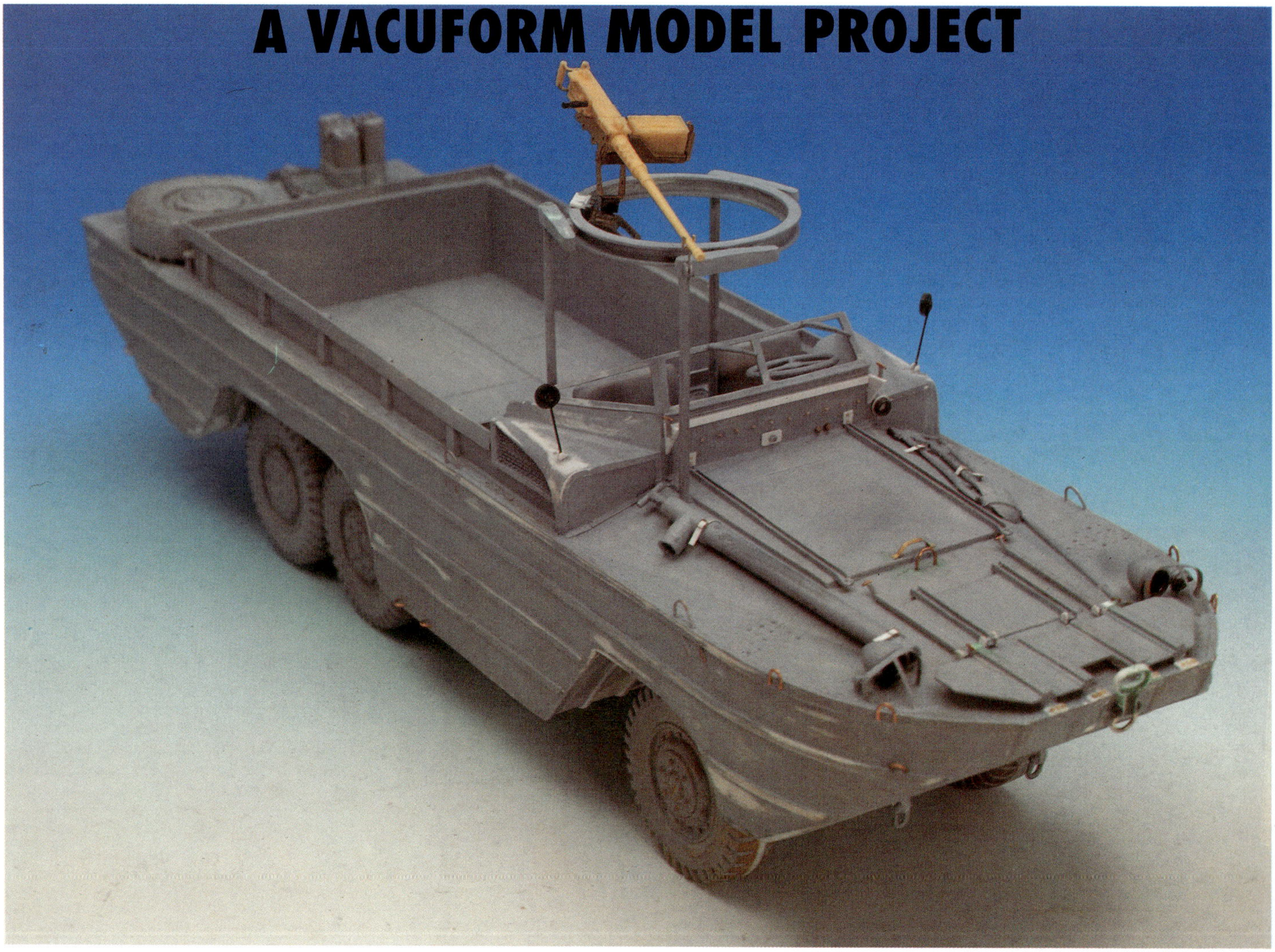

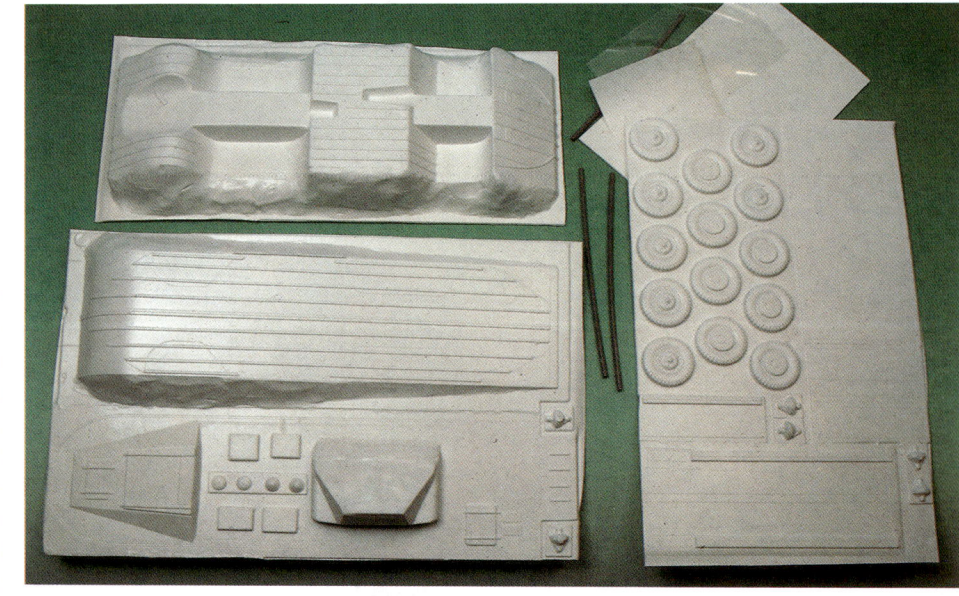

1/35 SCALE DUKW 6X6 AMPHIBIOUS TRUCK

Plastic models appear on the market with relentless regularity and hardly a month seems to pass without there being something new in the shops. Nowadays the quality of these kits is generally very high, with a substantial price tag. Cheaper options are limited although a vacuformed kit should not be as expensive as the latest offering from the mainstream injection moulded kit manufacturers. Building a vacuform does not take that much more time than a conventional kit and the final result should be just as good. A degree of scratchbuilding is

Pressed into carrier sheets, vacuform kit parts have first to be cut out.

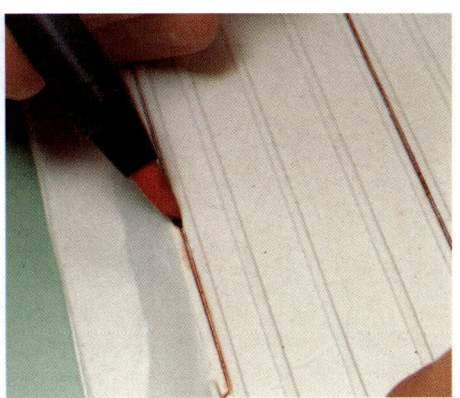

A marking pen is used to draw around the parts to allow a small extra area for trimming.

Large items can be cut out with scissors but again a small margin is advisable.

Straight pieces can be cut with a rule and sharp bladed knife or scalpel.

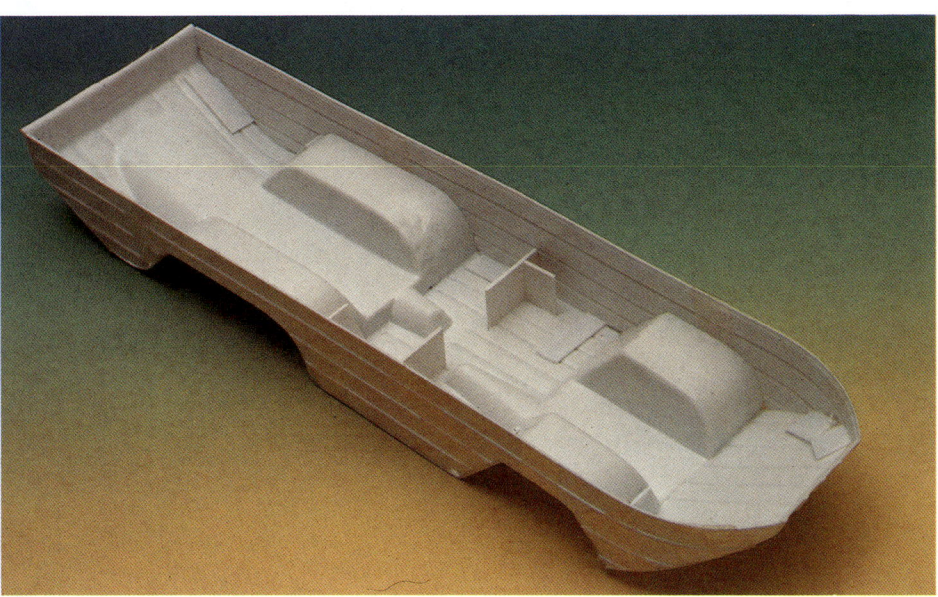

The vehicle hull is separated from the chassis and the edges smoothed down with file and sandpaper.

often necessary with these kits, particularly where smaller items such ashinges lack inherent strength due to the flimsy nature of vacuformed plastic. Take heart - custom building provides useful experience for subsequent, more ambitious model projects.

STARTING ASSEMBLY

All vacuform models come on one or more 'flat' white carrier sheets with the model parts stamped in relief. Each item has to be cut out of the carrier sheet with knife or scissors, a task that can present some problems as the white plastic does not always offer

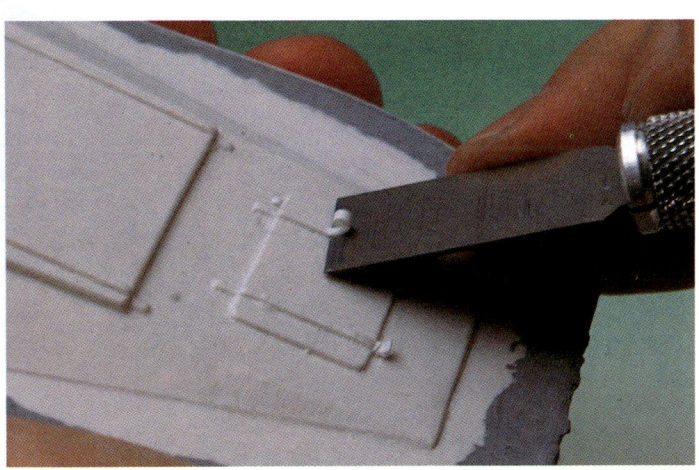

Some corners of vacuform kits are weak and need reinforcing to ensure good joints.

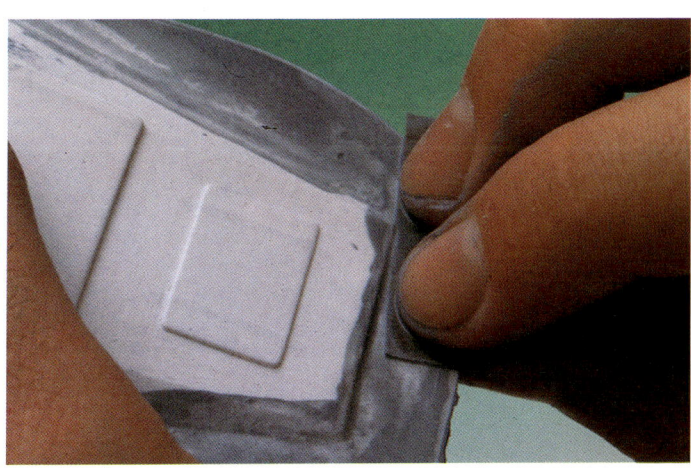

The join between the hull and deck sections should be firmly glued and sanded and any gaps filled with body putty.

Oversize rivets and crude detail that is to be refined later is removed at this stage.

Putty should be applied to any area that needs filling.

Any oversize holes may be plugged with epoxy resin.

a good contrast along the edges of the component parts. It is a good idea to highlight the exact area of each part with a fine marker pen before starting to cut it out. A small overlap along each edge is advisable for trimming off later with file or sandpaper.

Despite the degree of detail achieved with vacuforms, many very small items in scale size are too weak to use. Glue the main components with regular polystyrene cement or cyanoacrolate. Liquid adhesives allow a little more flexibility if any repositioning of parts is required during assembly.

Because vacuform plastic parts are much lighter than polystrene ones it is usually necessary to impart rigidity by adding strength on the inside of a vehicle. This is done by constructing a framework or box structure built up from 0.5-mm plastic card, the extent of this interior reinforcement depending on the type of model. By making the basic structure stronger, any patching or filling necessary as a

Flimsy parts and weak corners are reinforced with sections of plastic strip.

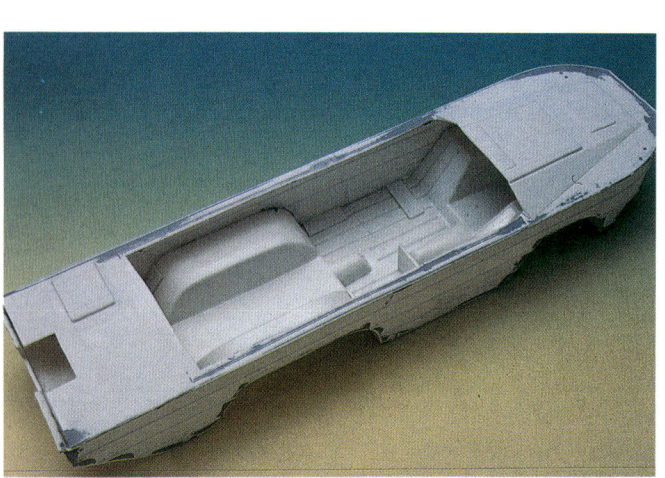

Care must be taken to ensure that vehicle box sections and other main sub-assemblies are exactly aligned before they are glued together.

result of a mistake when cutting the parts from the carrier sheet can be rectified with filler or plastic strip patching. Sanding down and finishing is then carried out as with any other plastic kit.

Before assembling a major component such as a turret to a tank hull, ensure that the interior strengtheners do not cause any obstruction. Small strengthener strips can of course be added to the inner faces of most components.

MAIN MATERIALS: HOW TO MAKE RIVETS

Making rivets look realistic is a perpetual problem with AFV kits. Sections of stretched plastic sprue inserted into shallow drill holes is a reliable enough method. The protruding heads are then sanded down to a round section. The danger here is that the base plastic might be crazed so working with thin metal sheet might be preferable. The hole and sprue method can be used with aluminium or brass sheet but an alternative is to

A hole smaller than the new rivet head is drilled out.

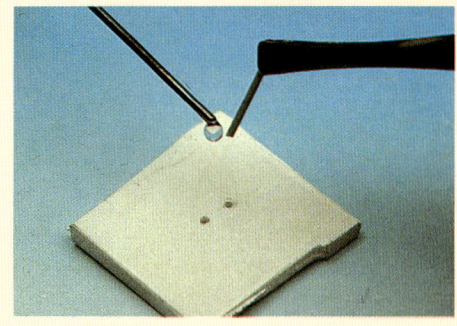

A drop of glue is applied over the hole and allowed to dry.

Melted plastic sprue also makes convincing rivets to the correct size.

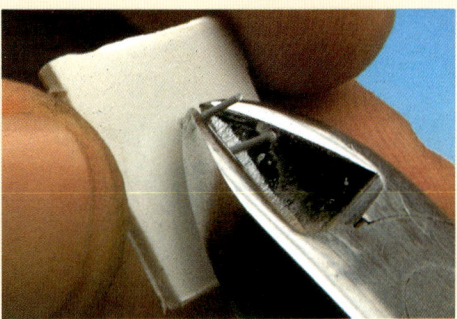

The melted sprue 'strings' are methodically cut off.

When working with sheet metal a small soldering iron will speed up the work.

The plastic melts in a semi-circlular shape.

Holes being made in 3/10 in alumimium sheet.

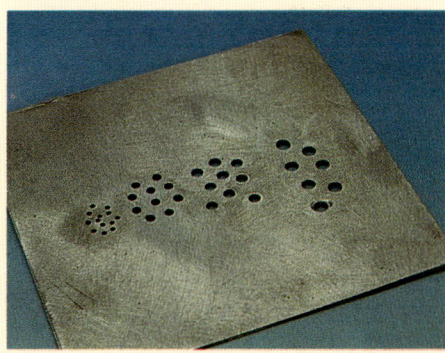

Small holes of different diameter will need grouping closely.

Heating the end of a drill helps it penetrate the plastic.

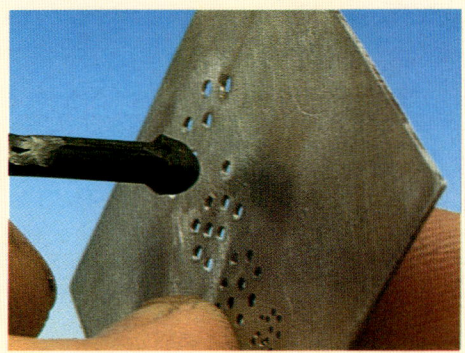

Chosing the kind of rivets that need to be reproduced.

Push the plastic strip into the hole until it protrudes through.

The shape is neatly formed by trimming the end.

Sand to form the rounded rivet head.

Prepared rivets should be carefully stored until use.

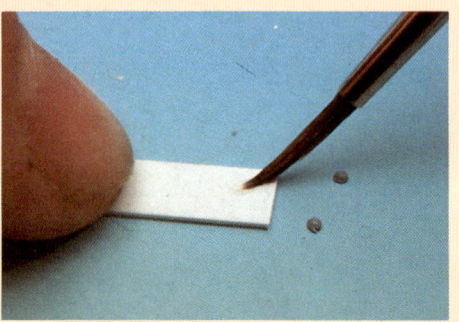

Apply liquid glue with the tip of a paintbrush.

Pick up the rivet with a moistened paintbrush.

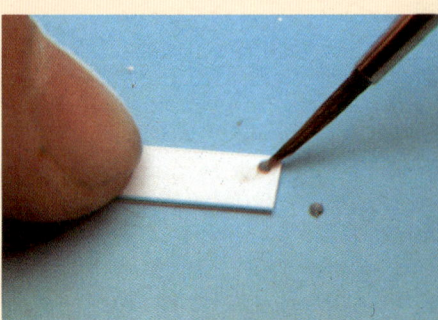

Use a separate brush to that reserved for glue application.

With the methods described many rivets can be made in several sizes.

A more traditional method is to use rivet heads from other kits.

melt the sprue and progressively 'print' the rivets as drops of molten plastic onto the sheet at previously marked intervals.

DETAILING THE MODEL

With the main bodywork of the vacuform DUKW assembled and the necessary corrective work carried out, the detailing process can begin. The reader will not

Pencil lines will help you apply the rivets in straight rows.

Refer constantly to reference material and plans before applying the new rivets.

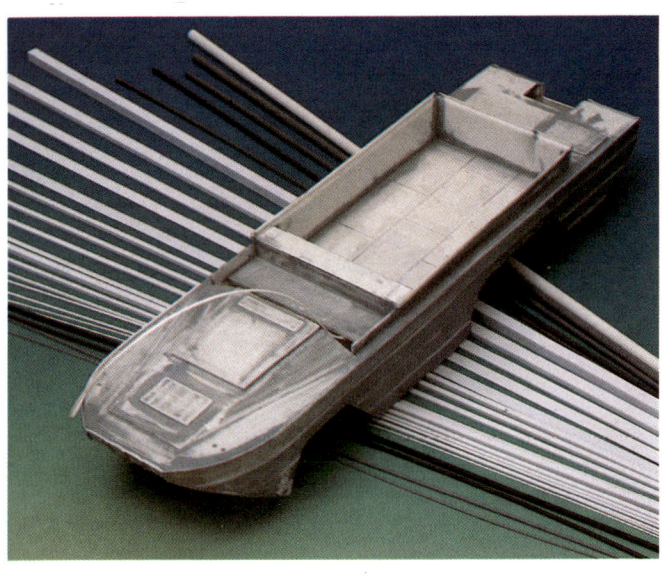

A stage of the work invariably helped by a selection of plastic strip, squares, rod and tubing in different sizes.

Strip is highly flexible and can be cut or folded with ease.

have failed to notice that this model has combined boat and vehicle characteristics and therefore there will be references to some parts that have a distinctly nautical flavour.

Have a range of plastic strips, rods and tubing to hand, not forgetting tube cement and liquid adhesive. Don't think that we are advising that the modeller makes everything from scratch, as other kit parts will be incorporated wherever possible.

Thin lengths of strip need to be glued across the upper horizontal part of the hull; being highly flexible, plastic strip will bend easily around curves. In the front section of the lower part of the hull a base is prepared to take the trailer rings. It will also be noted that the bay

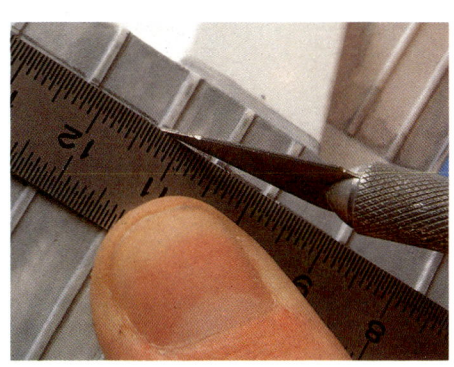

Gluing on the basic pieces of the trailer ring.

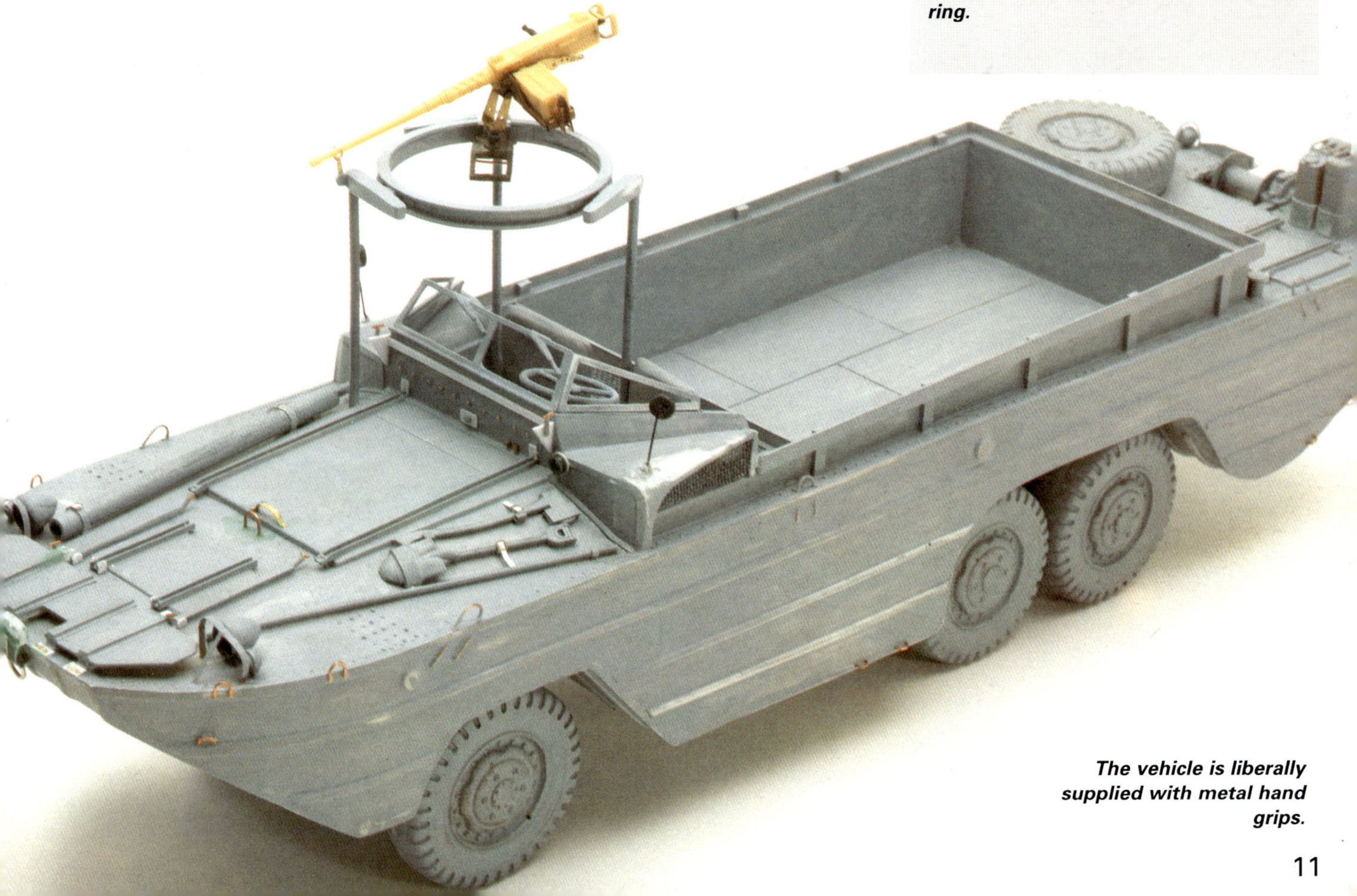

The vehicle is liberally supplied with metal hand grips.

11

The baseplate for the front axle is too high and should be set at a slight angle.

After cutting the base and removing some kit detail, reinforce with plastic squares.

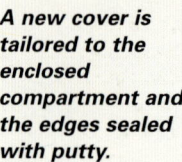

A new cover is tailored to the enclosed compartment and the edges sealed with putty.

The deck area is sanded and the divisions marked out.

On the top of the box section, lateral plastic strips are applied.

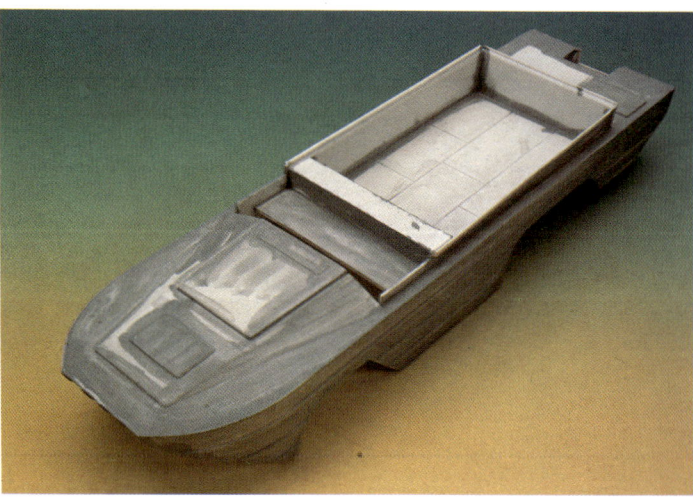

The strip that forms the base of the box has more strips applied laterally.

Each vertical plastic strip reinforcement is aligned with its hole, with the largest at the rear.

where the front axle is located does not have the correct dimensions. Remove the kit-moulded bay and either pare it down with a knife or make a new one from customised plastic squares to build up the base support for a plastic load-bearing bar fixed to the axle. Putty is used to fill any holes.

The load-bearing bar is divided into several sections. The necessary grooves should be well defined with a scalpel blade or triangular file and well cleaned out

Behind the cabin is an exhaust outlet which should be built with plastic strip and grille sections following plans of the DUKW.

when the work is completed. Grooves in the bar (from 1-mm rod) are best drawn out first. All the walls in this bay together with reinforcements, are made from plastic sheet and strip. As with many tasks of this nature, a metal rule and sharp scalpel blade make for clean cuts.

The vacuform parts include items such as the differential which due to the moulding process, is

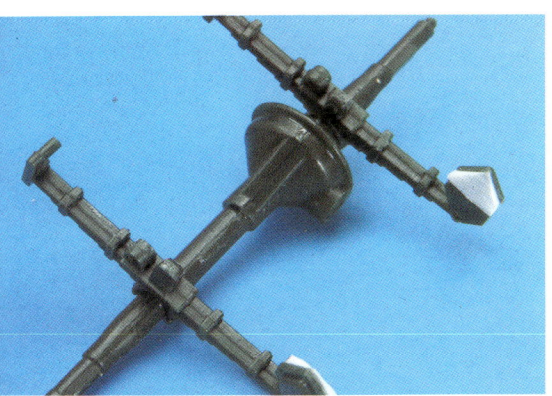

The front axle comes from an Italeri GMC 6 x 6 truck kit and needs a plastic rod support.

The springs are fixed to longitudinal beams.

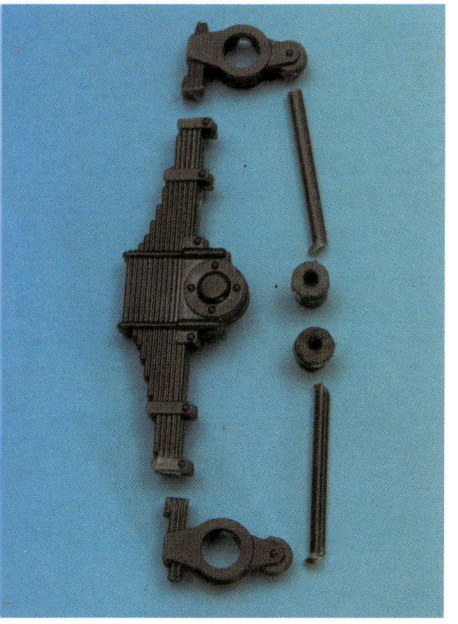

Springs must be lengthened slightly and thicker steering rods added.

Assembly of both axles is aided by central supports from plastic rod with tubing providing a new driveshaft.

Wheel moulding using Maskol reinforced with plaster.

neither as detailed or as strong as desirable. For this particular project transmission parts were borrowed from an Italeri GMC cargo truck kit. Modifications to tailor the front axle to the DUKW are minimal and the springs only need enlarging slightly with the help of plasticard.

The rear axle is a little more complex in that not only do the

BUILDING THE WHEELS

Altering the wheels may offer the biggest challenge in building this particular DUKW model. The wheels provided are not sufficiently detailed and although the Italeri truck kit provided some traction parts, the wheels themselves are too small. A deep spares box provided an alternative, namely

of making a wheel is to prepare a Maskol mould by gluing one Monogram wheel half to a hard surface. Cover this with six or seven further coats of Maskol and let it dry thoroughly. Finally, coat

springs need lengthening but the location points need attending to. Some of the drive train also needs to be made as do some inside parts of the vehicle chassis. Plastic tubing is ideal for this work and plastic rod can be cut to length to simulate the steering arms that connect the central axle and spring pivots.

Monogram's M-8 Greyhound kit. Although there are seven wheels in this old kit, the DUKW uses eight, so a copy has to made. The simplest - and cheapest - method

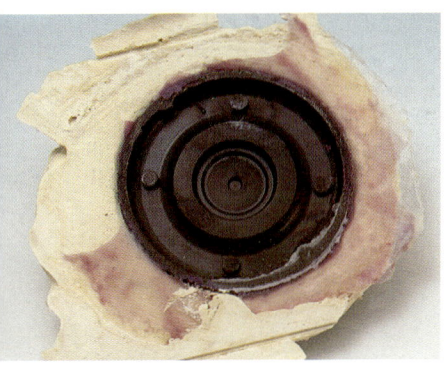

When the mould dries out the original wheel half remains.

There are many useful products available to make moulds including dental silicone.

Both parts of a wheel can be made using a silicone based filler.

Cut out a plastic disc to sandwich between the wheel halves.

Glue all three components together and sand as necessary.

The new widened wheels in position on their axle and spring arrangement.

Copper, brass, resin and vacuform moulding techniques combine to superdetail the DUKW kit.

the mould with modelling plaster to add rigidity.

When the Maskol mould is released, the plastic wheel half leaves a perfect female half which is then filled with resin, plaster or molten plastic - whichever method is preferred. The process is rather

slow as each time the filler is poured, it needs time to dry before adding the next one. A more expensive option is to use a filling material such as dentist's silicon solution. This will set quickly, enabling a job like this to be completed in about ten minutes.

When two wheel halves are to hand, cut out a hub strengthener and attach this before gluing both halves together. A final check on tyre size may result in some sanding down, but with this done, the wheel modification is all but complete and ready for attachment to the vehicle. The foregoing task will at least have provided the modeller

with some experience and patience - a commodity that can get shorter the longer the model takes!

PROPELLER AND RUDDER

Despite our considerable progress, this DUKW kit needs more work before it is completed. A useful tip is not to tackle all the necessary modifications at once but to leave the project for a day or so. Return to it fresh and your enthusiasm will surely have returned. Now for some of the final jobs.

In the rear interior of the DUKW are the devices that make this vehicle so versatile, a rudder and propeller. A new propeller will have to be found, perhaps by borrowing one from a naval ship kit. This is connected to a plastic rod drive shaft. Cut out the rudder and sand it to shape before attaching it to the hull with plastic strip.

Attention can now be focussed on the final assembly and addition of exterior details using both kit and custom-built components. The breakwater comes from the kit although the hinges and reinforcements sections that hold it onto the hull are new, fashioned from small

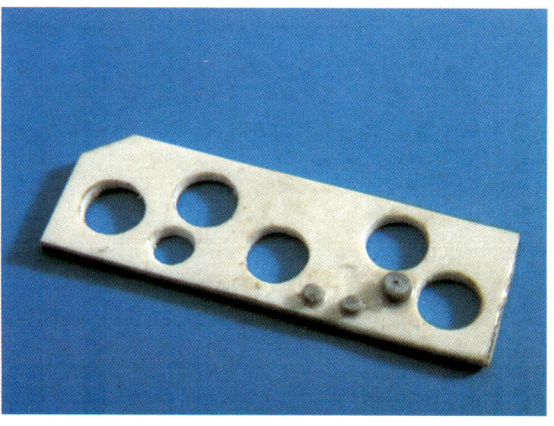

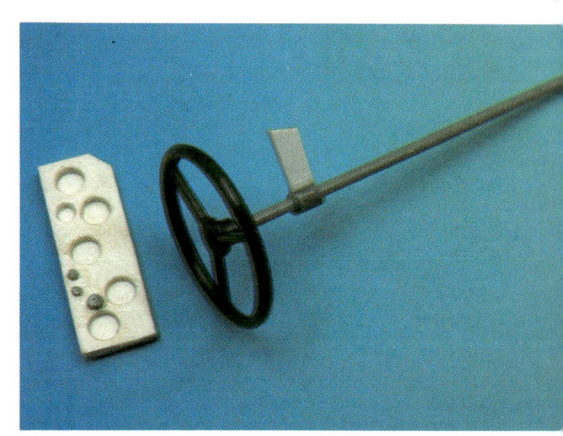

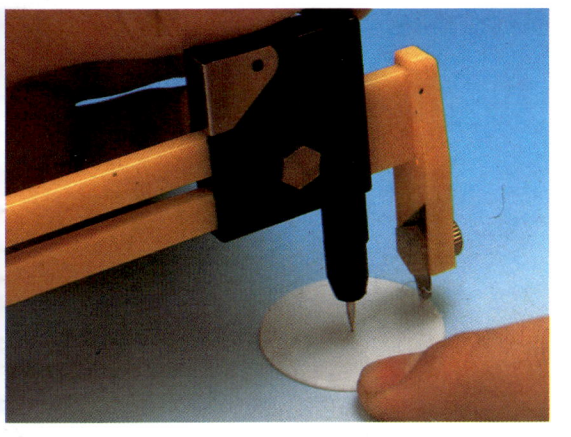

To add a mchine gun support ring a plastic circle needs to be made first.

A second ring is cut, sanded and added to the first.

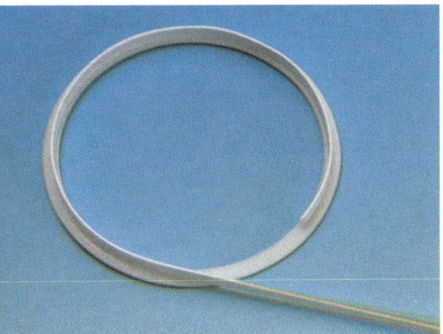

This second ring is added inside the first one.

The ring supports are made from plastic rod.

After painting, the instrument panel and steering wheel are positioned.

and a section of plastic or brass sheet with circular holes. This is of course an instrument dashboard which has gauges for temperature, oil pressure, fuel, engine revs and so forth. Mark out each instrument on plastic sheet and punch out a small hole that can then be enlarged with a file. Alternatively, if using a harder material such as brass, a drill nearer the correct size will virtually eliminate any need to clean up with a file.

MACHINE GUN SUPPORT

Many DUKWs had an elevated 0.50-calibre machine gun set on a circular ring above the driving position. Adding this to a model

offcuts of plastic strip. The ever-useful plastic strip is also used for any other external strengtheners that can be seen on the DUKW hull. The deck headlight comes from the Italeri truck kit, its guard being marked out as a strip on 3/10 thick brass, cut with scissors and bent to the desired shape. Fix this in position with cyanoacrolate.

Along the edge of the crew position there is work for a punch

Behind the driving seats are the panels covered by grilles which are glued with cryanoacrylate.

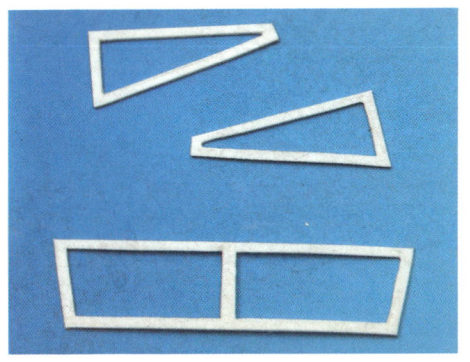

The kit windscreen panels were replaced by new ones cut from clear plastic sheet.

Make a test fit but leave these new panels until last.

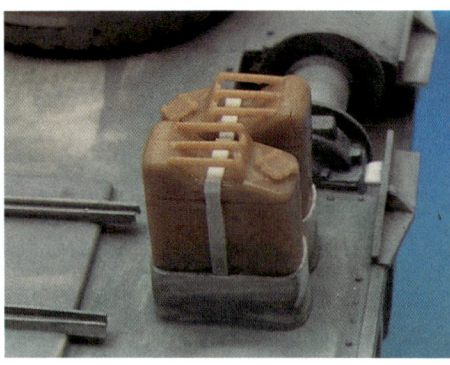

Jerrycans are located with thin plasticard supports at the base and around each can.

The rear headlight protectors are also fashioned from thin brass strip.

out two rings of the correct diameter onto plastic card sheet and cut them out ready for sandwiching together. When the adhesive is dry, sand the inside face of the ring smooth and set aside for positioning on the vertical posts. The machine gun barrel also needs a small stop attached to the traversing ring. As part of the finishing

process, the windscreen complete with clear plastic 'glass' provided in the kit, was carefully glued into position.

In the bow there is a mooring ring which is made in several sec-

provides some variety although this vacuform kit does not include armament. The weapon itself is easily found in an accessory kit but the mounting will have to be made from plastic sheet and rod. Mark

The hawser winch comes from an Italeri GMC truck kit while the supports are made from plastic, scaled from DUKW plans.

The simple bow coupling is made from shaped strips filled with putty.

Below the windscreen are tools held down by plastic and copper retainers.

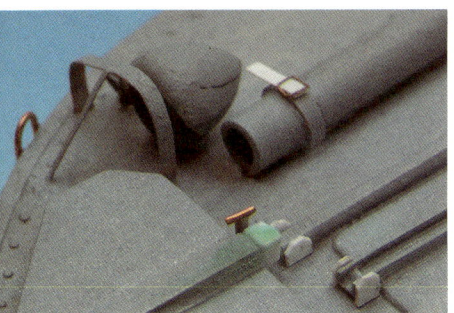

All external items are retained by clips or straps.

Putty filler provides strength and a good 'key' for painting.

The tool retaining straps have photoetch buckles.

DRAWING KEY

Fill with putty

Basic pieces

Shaped piece

Lateral reinforcements

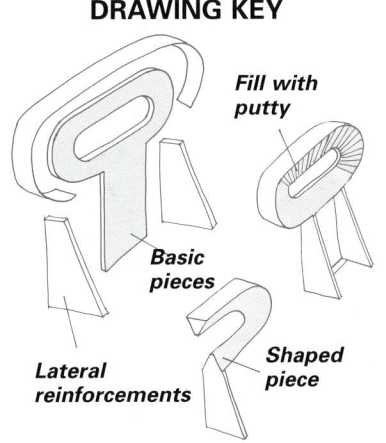

Along the hull edge are different sized handgrips made from copper wire.

Don't overlook the smaller handgrips situated on the lower hull.

The finished machine gun ring with its supports and stops made from shaped and sanded plastic pieces. The gun retainer is in brass.

tions filled with putty. The ring itself is copper strip, bent to shape. A numbr of tools are fastened to the deck by leather straps, all of which are made from plastic strip. The buckles are made from copper or are photoetch items from an accessory kit; other small brass components along the hull are positioned at this stage of the work. The last item to glue on is the machine gun ring sub-assembly, the culmination of a challenging conversion.

A VACUFORM AND MIXED MEDIA MODEL

Sd.Kfz.11

Traditionally, vacuforming has been used primarily to offer the modeller parts to make alternative versions of subjects released as injection moulded kits. We are going to combine parts of a Tamiya Sd.Kfz. 251/1 and 251/9 German WWII halftrack to make the Sd.Kfz.11 personnel carrier. In general the area where each vehicle differs the most are hidden, a fact that good scale plans that include as many profile views as possible, will soon reveal.

As it comes the Tamiya model has a number of areas that need attending to, including a short rear body. This has to be lengthened by 3-mm at a point just under the door. Height too has to be altered. Research will reveal that the mudguards are also too small and when enlarging these with epoxy

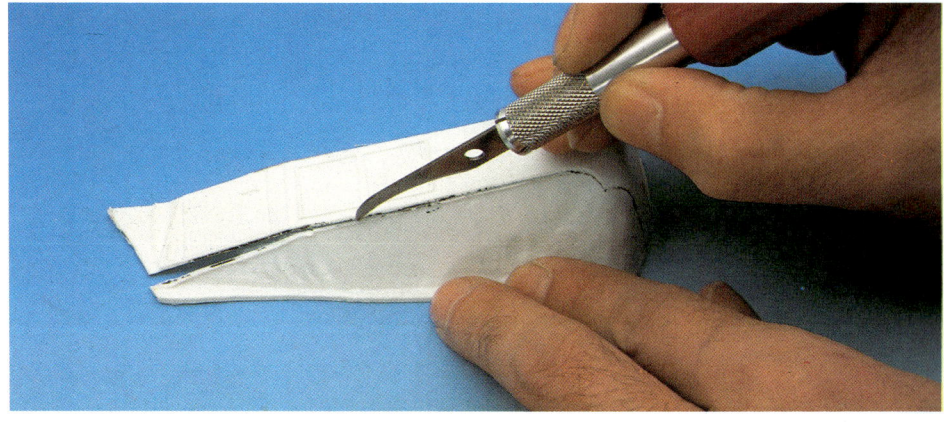

The first stage is to mark out new pieces with a fine pen.

A curved scalpel blade is ideal for cutting the plastic accurately.

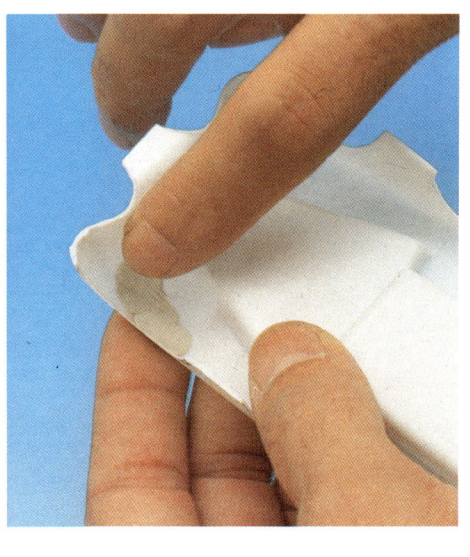

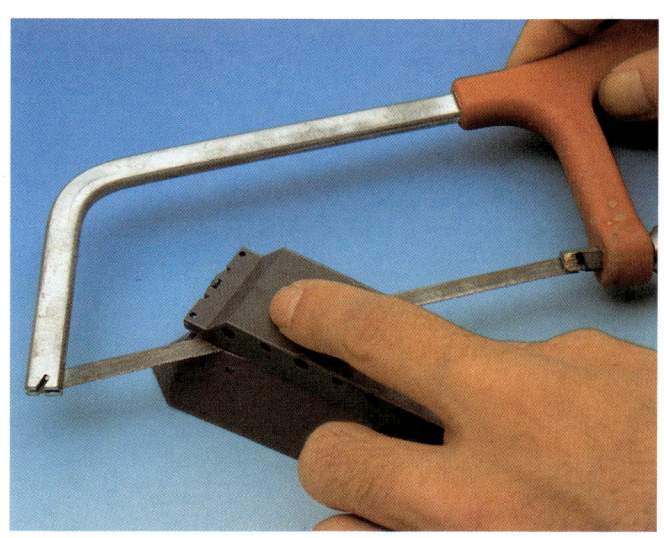

Epoxy putty is used to fill and reinforce the thin strips.

The lower part of the Sk. Kfz. 251/1 chassis has to be cut off for use in the conversion.

putty, corresponding modifications will have to be made to the chassis and body.

Any cutting of the injection moulded kit should be done with great care after carefully tracing the area out with a fine pen. Use a razorsaw or small hacksaw for this work, sanding the edges smooth and finishing with sandpaper.

Work is best carried out if the various areas are treated separately - chassis, mudguards and bodywork. Very small items such as the rear-view mirrors, steps and pennant posts are left until the model is virtually complete. To reproduce the seats thick (1.5-mm) plastic card is measured and cut in the right proportions after having drawn out the dimensions. Finishing with file and sandpaper will result in the desired effect, this stage even including adding some realistic-looking folds and rucks in the seat upholstery.

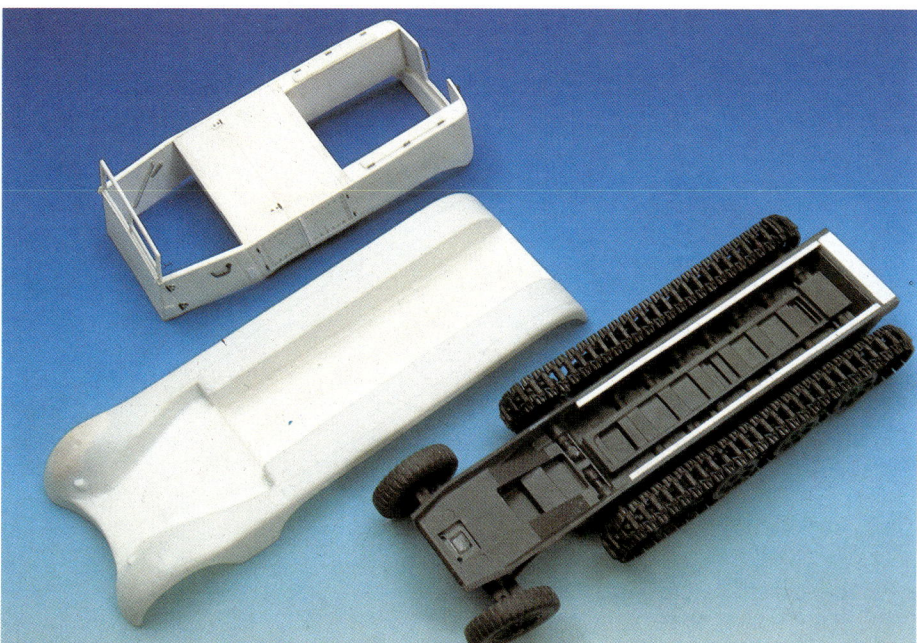

The three main components of the vehicle. The chassis is built up with plastic strip, the body has extra detailing in the form of hinges and hand-holds and the wood areas will have the grain brought out.

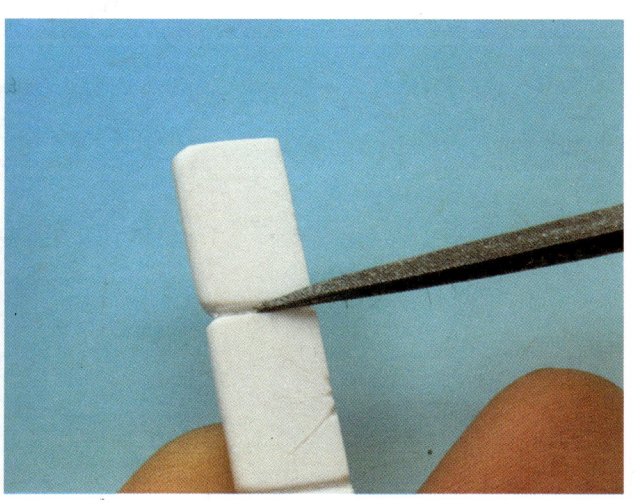

The seats are rebuilt from 1.5-mm plasticard, upholstery folds being added with a triangular file.

Round off the corners with a suitable abrasive.

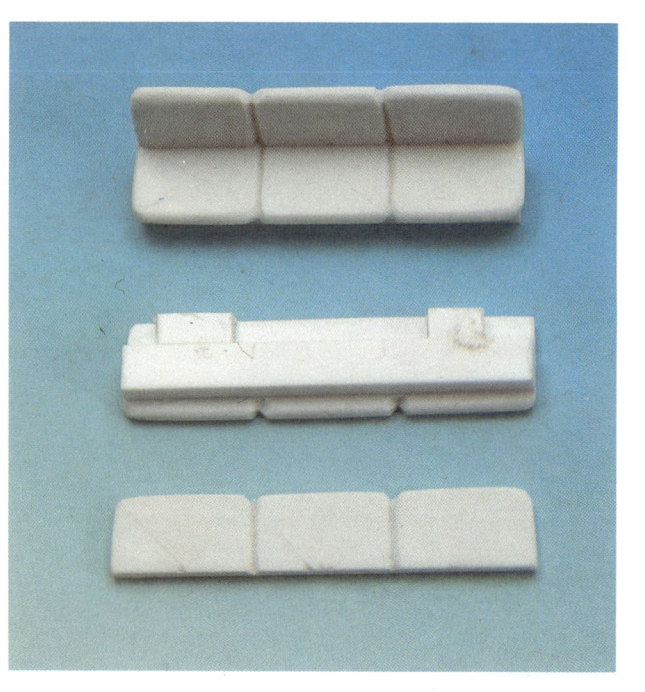

Each seat has two main sections, the base being mounted on a platform.

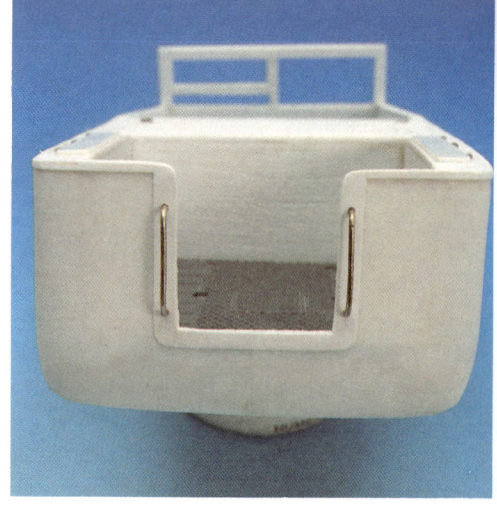

The rear door is reinforced with thin metal strips.

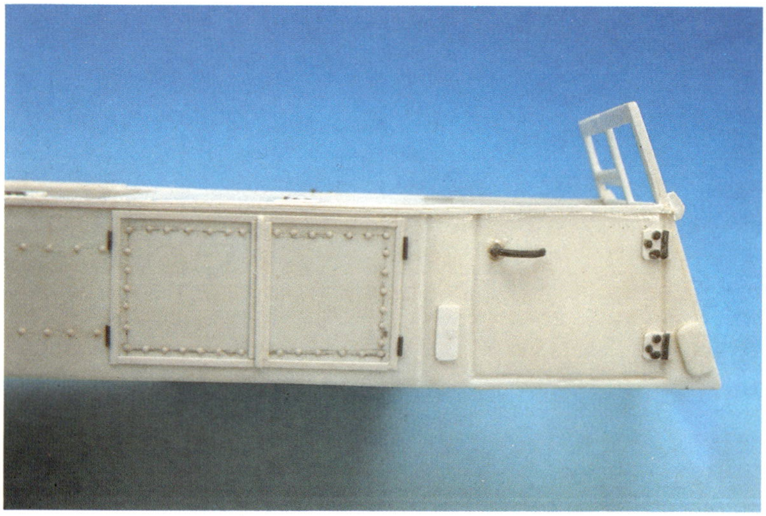

All the kit rivets need replacing following the described method and hinges and door furniture is added from plastic strip and rod.

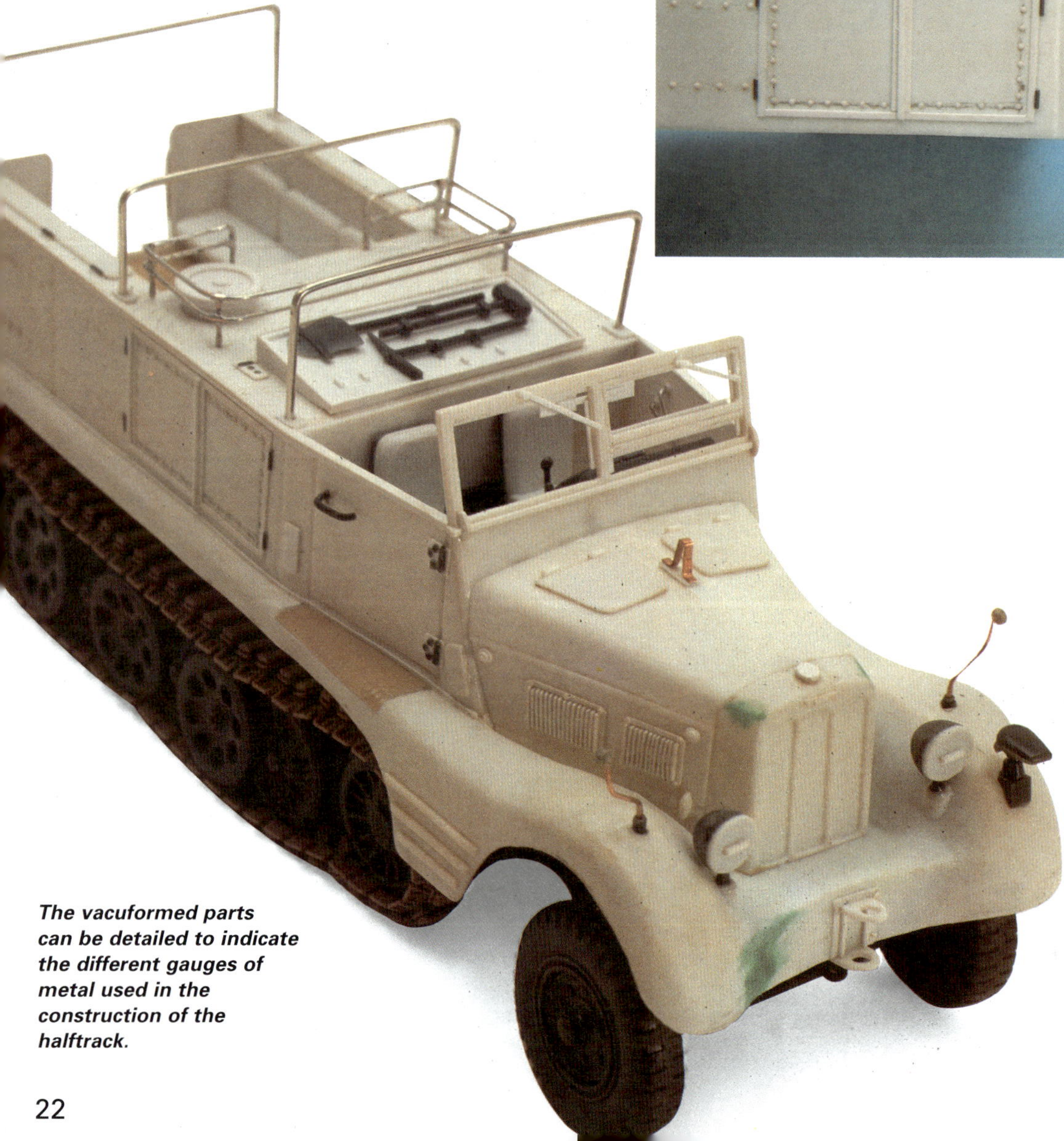

The vacuformed parts can be detailed to indicate the different gauges of metal used in the construction of the halftrack.

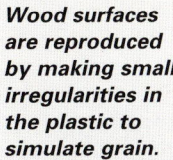

Windscreen parts must be cut and sanded to shape.

Wood surfaces are reproduced by making small irregularities in the plastic to simulate grain.

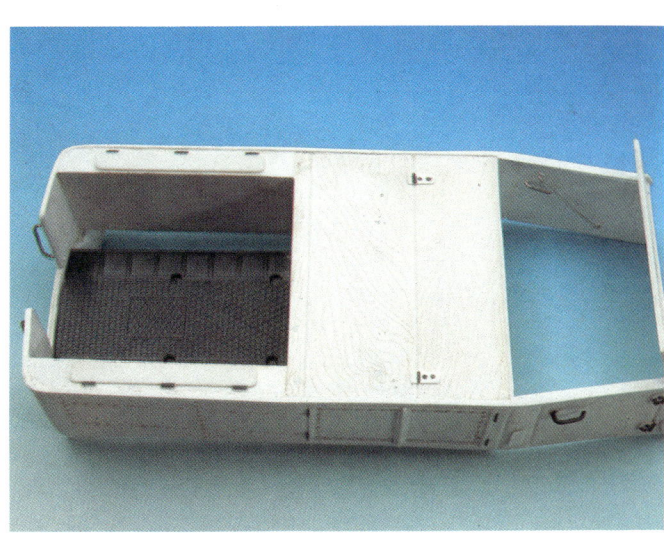

At each stage the extra detail added to the basic structure provides both 'depth' and realism.

The equipment bins are made out of metal strip using glue or solder for firm joints.

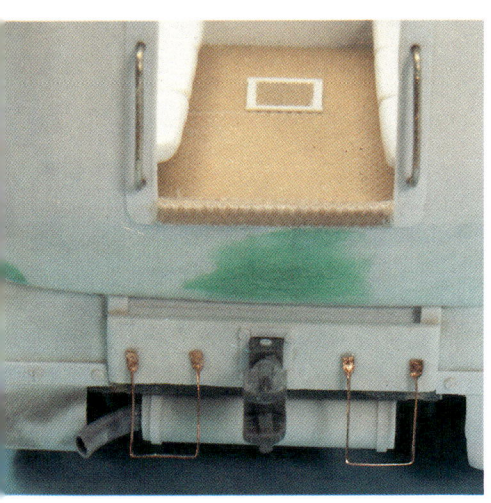

The exhaust and silencer are made from plastic tubing, the footrest from metal strip.

All the vehicle floor areas are covered in non-slip material, as described elsewhere.

SUPER-DETAILING

The detailing process takes in the entire vehicle and includes making sure that the prominent rivets are correctly spaced. To do this first draw a continuous line along the rivets, marking the correct spacing against a metal rule. Rivets are made in the same way as described in previous chapters and glued on one by one, carefully checking alignment and reinforcing with a drop of polystyrene cement where this might be needed. All hinges, door frames and reinforcement strips on the full size halftrack should also be reproduced in miniature.

Care should be taken with hanging the doors; their hinges are made from plastic rod. The windscreen should be cut out neatly and sanded to shape, kit parts being discarded in favour of new parts where necessary. Small items

The cooling louvres on the side of the bonnet are from very thin plastic strip placed in position and separated by spacers.

A view of the cab with the dashboard and steering wheel in position.

The finished model requires some modelling ability but intelligent use of plans and photographs makes this project, which combines standard kit parts with easy to make custom parts, relatively straightforward and satisfying.

such as the windscreen wipers should be added from brass wire, the tiny wiper motors being made from plastic blocks. To make the canvas cover strong enough, shape the supports from copper wire and use this material for the handgrips and footrests. Storage bins are made out of plastic strip and wire, the latter material being soldered rather than glued for a really strong joint. Non-slip material needs adding to floor areas and the mudguards.

The Tamiya kit's transmission, steering wheel and instrument panel dials can be used in this conversion.

VEHICLE INTERIORS

More detail is now being added to vehicle kits, particularly
those cast in resin, and a wide range of customising parts sets are
available to improve the look of engines, drives,
axles and turrets. But there are still additional items that the modeller
can add, usually by scratch-building.
To show off the work done, start off with tank or AFV kits which
allow a view of the interior through doors and hatches
when the vehicle is complete.
A stage further leads naturally to something more ambitious such as
tackling the inside of a World War I German A7V tank,
progressing to more elaborate work utilising parts produced by your
own moulding techniques.

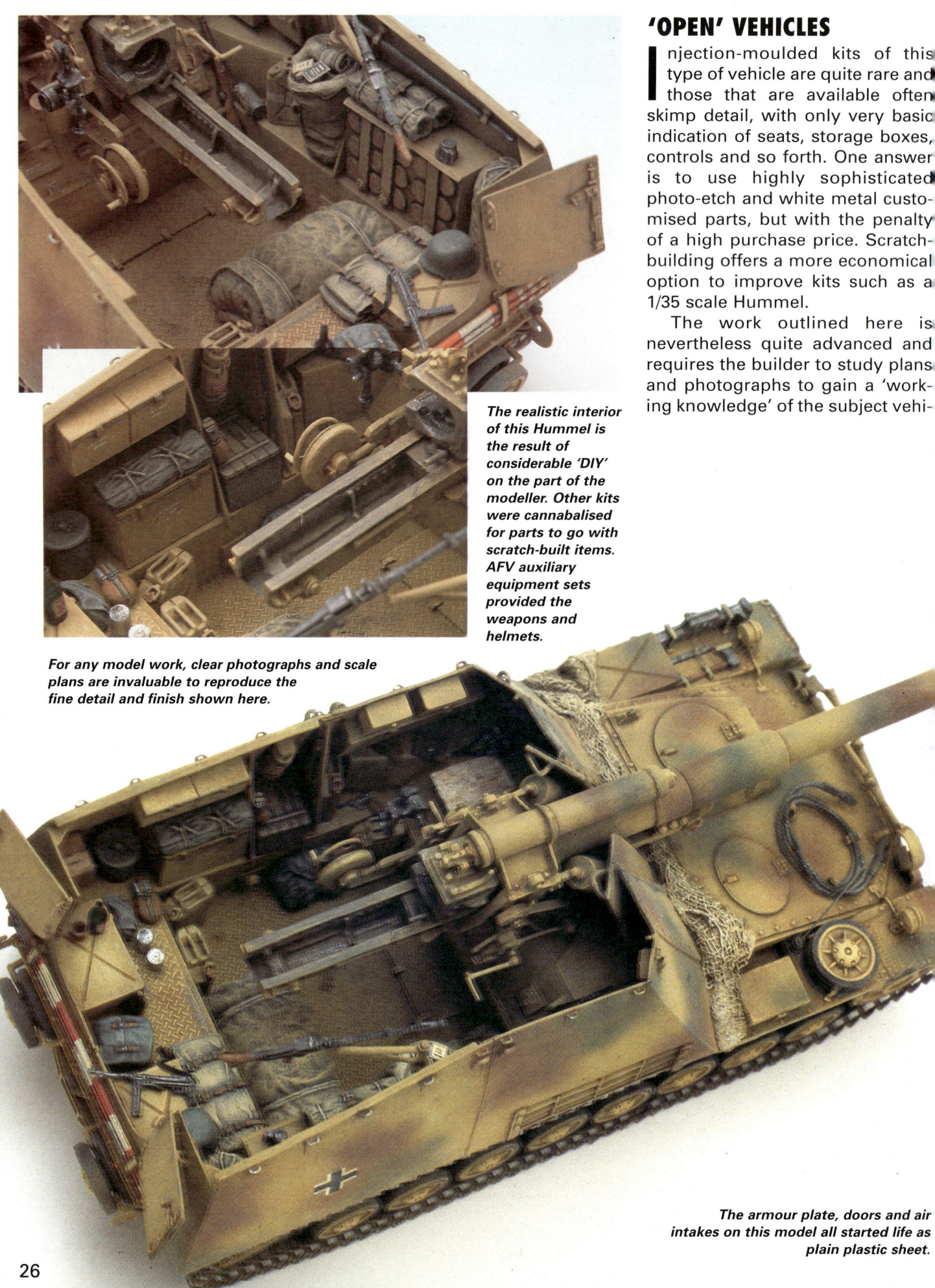

'OPEN' VEHICLES

Injection-moulded kits of this type of vehicle are quite rare and those that are available often skimp detail, with only very basic indication of seats, storage boxes, controls and so forth. One answer is to use highly sophisticated photo-etch and white metal customised parts, but with the penalty of a high purchase price. Scratch-building offers a more economical option to improve kits such as a 1/35 scale Hummel.

The work outlined here is nevertheless quite advanced and requires the builder to study plans and photographs to gain a 'working knowledge' of the subject vehi-

The realistic interior of this Hummel is the result of considerable 'DIY' on the part of the modeller. Other kits were cannabalised for parts to go with scratch-built items. AFV auxiliary equipment sets provided the weapons and helmets.

For any model work, clear photographs and scale plans are invaluable to reproduce the fine detail and finish shown here.

The armour plate, doors and air intakes on this model all started life as plain plastic sheet.

cle. Fortunately, tanks and AFVs do not generally contain equipment with complex shapes, so square, rectangular and tubular sections made of plastic and other suitable materials can be adapted for most of the extras needed for the model. This brings into play unusual 'domestic' items such as pens, needles, plastic food packaging and vacuform mouldings. Mixing scales is also possible with certain items from other kits - the extent of detail incorporated is limited only by the individual modeller's imagination and skill. Some tasks will of course, require a fairly extensive range of tools.

This Panther tank's engine includes parts fashioned from stretched sprue, plastic sheet, copper wire and paper. The latter is coated with white glue and a very thin liquid putty solution to retain rigidity. Paper, which is invariably 'in scale', cuts easily and bonds well with adhesives.

BUILDING ENGINES

Detail sets for AFVs do not always extend to engines and for this 1/25 scale Panther tank, the powerplant was completely rebuilt. In this case paper rather than plastic sheet was used, the advantage being that paper can be easier to work with and the end result is much the same with either material. Paper also has a useful scale thickness, any lack of rigidity being restored by a thin coat of white glue; when dry this can be built up with liquid putty in the same manner as plastic. If tubes and couplings have to be made by building up plastic strip, one compensation is that there are many useful tools intended for 1/24 scale kits.

DETAILING THE INTERIOR

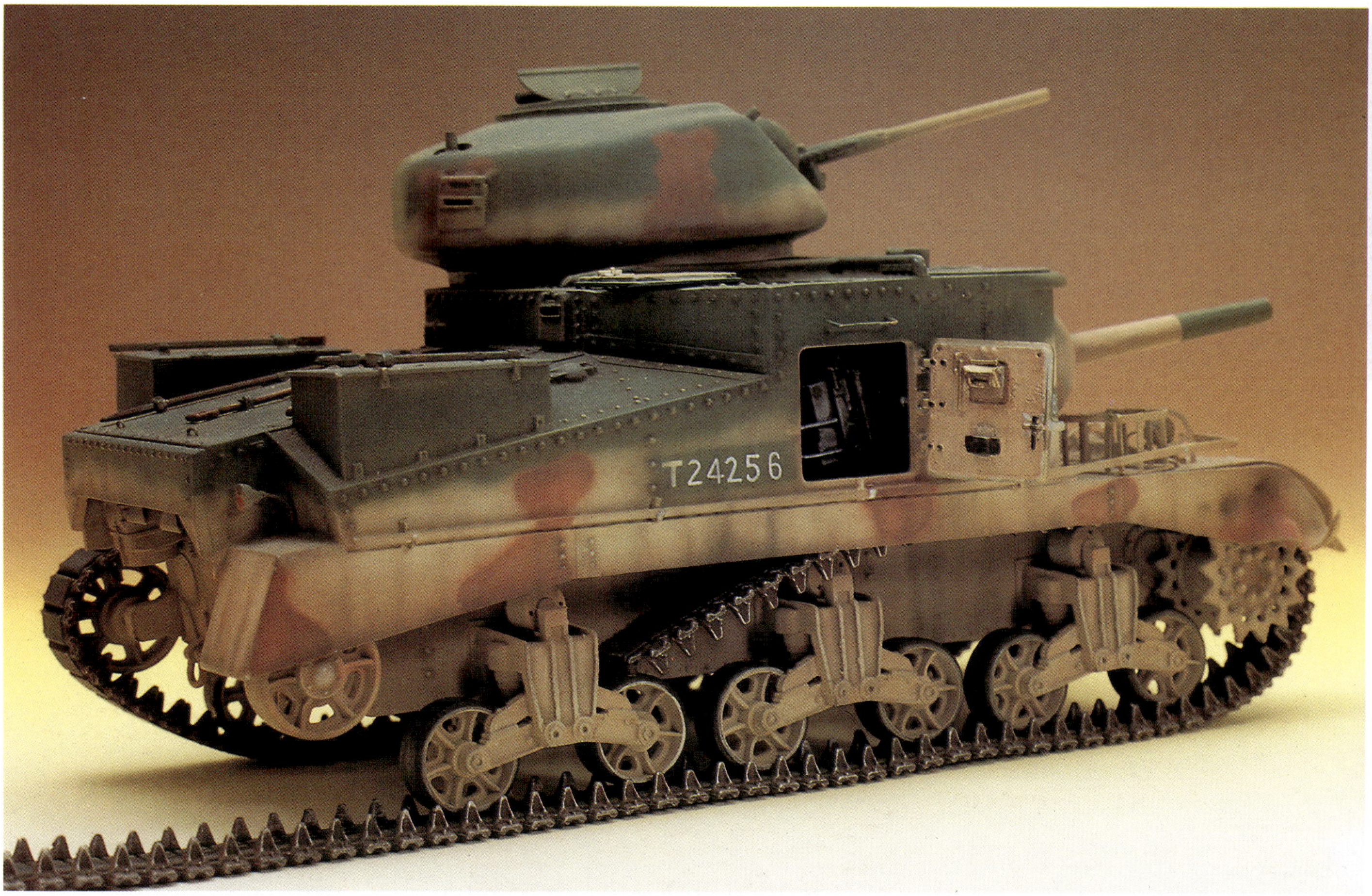

GENERAL GRANT TANK IN 1/35 SCALE

Most injection moulded kits of tanks do not provide interior detail and even if this is added, virtually the only way to view it is to have the vehicle all but destroyed, with large sections, such as the turret, missing. The General Grant by Tamiya offers the modeller some advantage in this respect by having a sizeable crew entry door which can be displayed open to show the interior.

Before construction starts it is useful to study plans and photographs of the full size tank. Our choice for this subject was the Osprey Vanguard volume No 9, The Lee/Grant Tanks in British Service. In building the kit we wanted to concentrate on those sections that can be seen through the hatches, including the am-

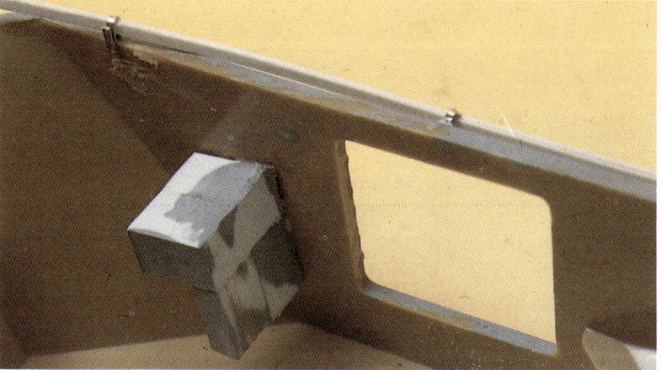

Large extra sections must be made out of plastic sheet using body putty to fill any gaps.

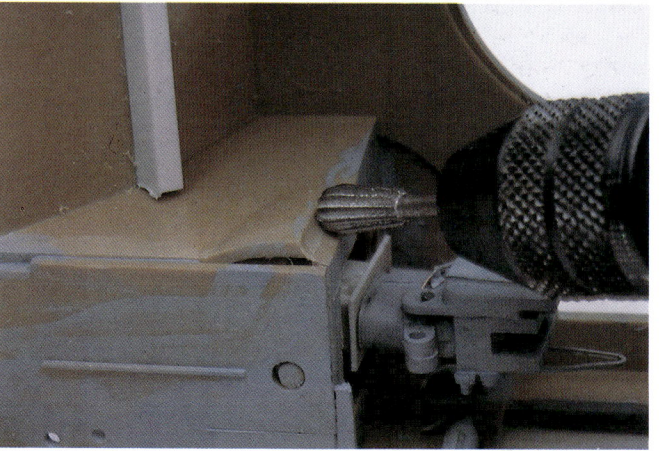

Various tools will be employed to complete the detail. Here a milling tool is used to ream out the area adjacent to the gun barrel.

REBUILDING THE BREECH

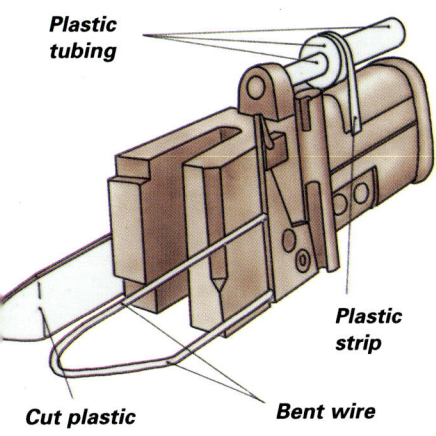

Plastic tubing

Cut plastic

Plastic strip

Bent wire

adapted from a Tamiya model of a British 6-pounder artillery piece, which had similar dimensions, items such as the recovery cylinders being made out of different thicknesses of plastic rod. The gunner's seat also needs to be

munition stowage area and gun barrel breech. The correct dimensions are first measured on plans taking account of the door size, which becomes the available 'viewing area'. These are then traced onto 0.4-mm plasticard. To carry out the necessary conversion work, a range of tools will be required, especially drills. Other detail areas which are borne in mind include adding some 75-mm shells from any kit which has these in the right size for this scale.

Basically, the Grant's hull gun breech was located in a vertical carrier block. This, the cylinder head and the armour plate surrounding the breech, all have to be built from scratch, as does the vertical pipe set in the floor to the left of the gun. Firstly, cut the wall of the model to take a base for the barrel. The gun itself can be

With the floor removed the new ammunition boxes, water bottles and seats can be seen.

Only those areas that are visible require extra detail, as this view of the hull emphasises.

scratch-built from plastic strip and sheet, with the cushions fashioned from epoxy putty. The revolving turret is fixed into a cylindrical well that stretches from the turret base to the floor of the tank. This well which requires cutting circular pieces at top and bottom, can be made from plastic sheet, tin or brass. Inside the well can be seen a seat, batteries and the 37-mm

The revolving turret and its entry door are made from plastic card or thin metal sheet.

ammunition stowage. The batteries are made out of plastic squares with some short rods and stretched sprue for the terminals and wiring. Sections of rod pointed at one end provide the shells and plasticard is again employed to construct the seat, which needs a cylindrical support framework and a cushion built up from putty.

The floor of the Grant, like most operational tanks, was littered with ammunition cases, tool boxes and food containers; items such as knapsacks containing gas masks and other equipment were stored beneath the crew seats. Fire extinguishers can also be made from plastic tubing and a box with a hinged lid holds the first-aid kit.

Racks for water bottles can be positioned on the wall of the turret well.

Gunner's seat and extra 37-mm shells around the walls of the turret well.

The Grant tank interior need only be basically equipped with as much equipment as the modeller prefers.

Gun breech detail in the upper part of the hull. Some 75-mm shells made from plastic tubing can be added for effect here.

A realistic gun breech can be built up without difficulty.

The recoil cylinder and hand grips add a final touch of realism.

None of these items is difficult to create out of basic plasticard and tube pieces and the end result certainly improves the finished model. Detail can be added to the inside of the doors, which were padded to offer some protection for the crew. Add the padding with a square of putty. This material can also be utilised for the sight cover. The gun breech is detailed with brass and hypodermic needle sections, a final touch being the inclusion of the hydraulic cables at the end of the breech of the 37-mm gun.

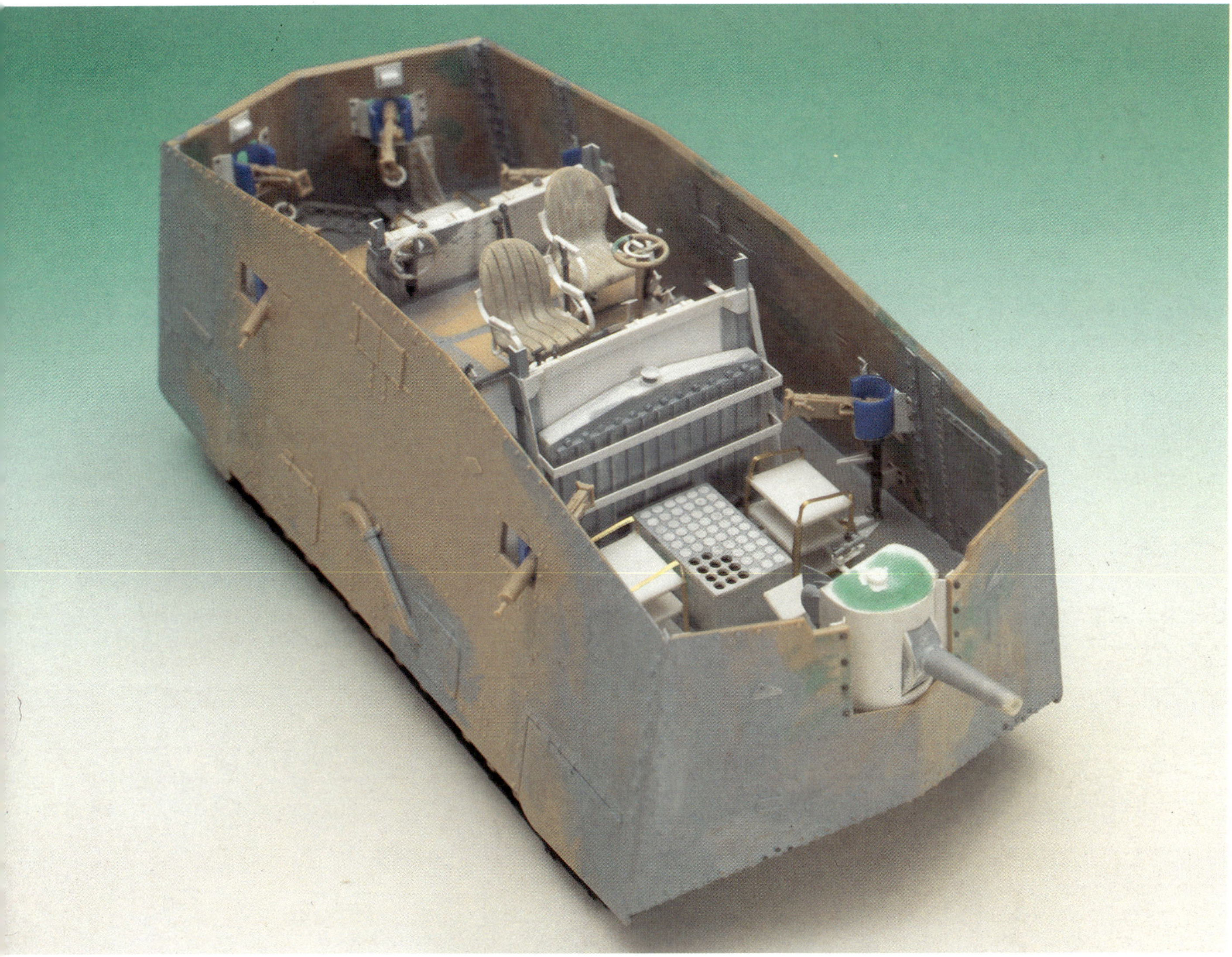

TOTAL INTERIOR REBUILD

A7V in 1/35 scale

Since it appeared many years ago this Tauro model represented a big challenge for modellers as the 'state of the art' was not well advanced. The open interior of the vehicle presented many possibilities for detailing but it was not until reliable data such as offered by the German Podzun Pallas-Verlag publications and the Waffen Arsenal series became available, that modellers had much to go on in this respect. Clear photographs of how the A7V looked made any work on the model that much easier. To the book references was added, in September 1990, an article in the magazine Model covering the

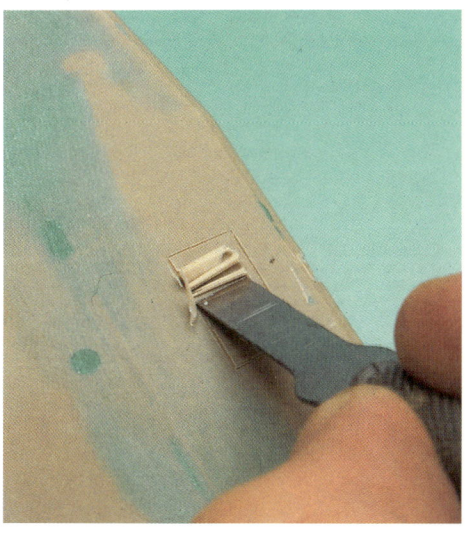

Moulded interior detail of the kit should be removed prior to rebuilding.

rebuilding of a full size A7V for museum display. As the article also included a scale plan it was clearly time to dust off the Tauro model and get started!

COMPLETE REBUILDING

After studying the references you rapidly conclude that the only usable kit items are the machine guns and possibly the control wheel. This means that everything else, including the interior walls, need to be replaced. Using the techniques previously described you need a compass, a range of punches in different diameters, some brass mouldings and plastic sheet, strips and squares. To reproduce rivets, perforated sheet

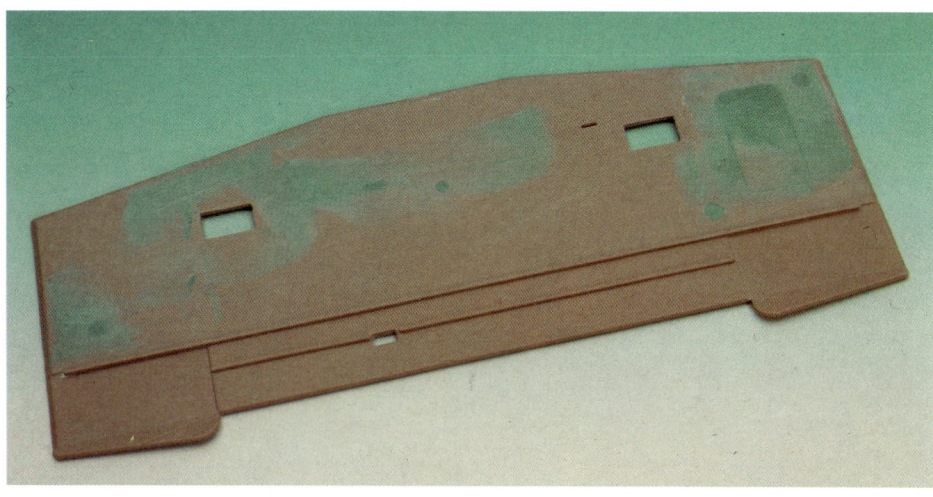

New components are scaled, drawn out and filled with green putty as appropriate.

metal used in conjunction with heated plastic is ideal, 3/10 thick brass sheeting also being used for other items.

Start by removing the interior detail moulded into the kit walls with a sharp knife or suitable file and fill the resulting gaps with body putty. The scribed lateral gun hatches can be emphasised and deepened with a knife but in our case we entirely rebuilt the plate walls that incorporate these. The rear entry hatch with its reinforced iron strips and rivets was also rebuilt. Don't forget to reposition the hatch hinges in the right place! Rivets, hatch surrounds and reinforement strips are reproduced

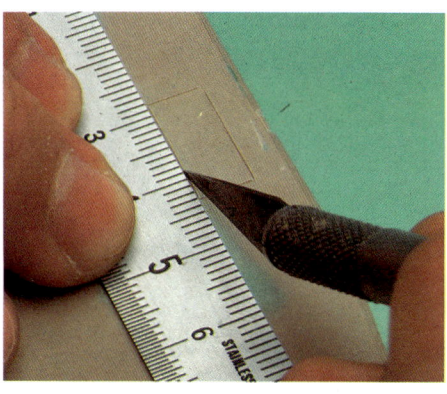

New forward appertures should be cut from card.

Our model has no obervation hatches in the front section and those moulded in the kit should be removed.

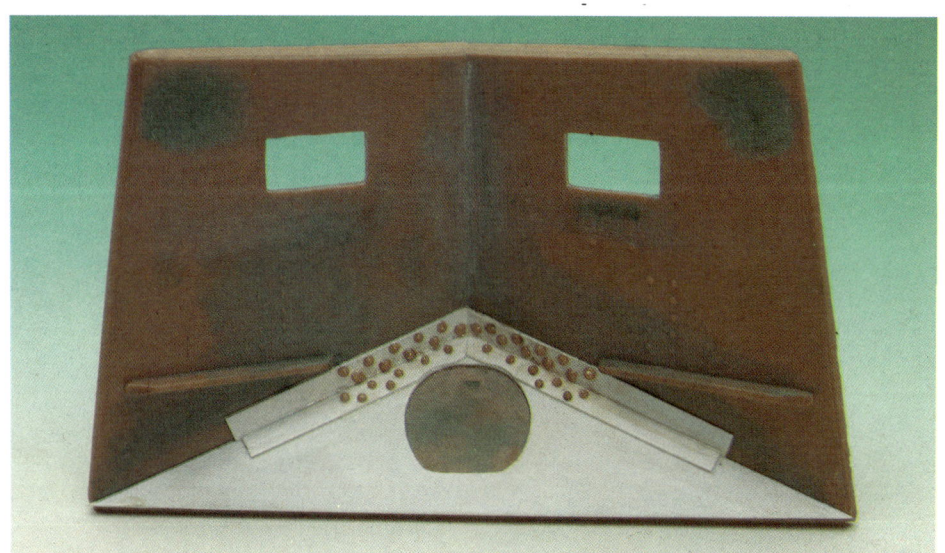

In the rear of the A7V there is an entry hatch and a riveted metal sheet held in position by a 'V' angle.

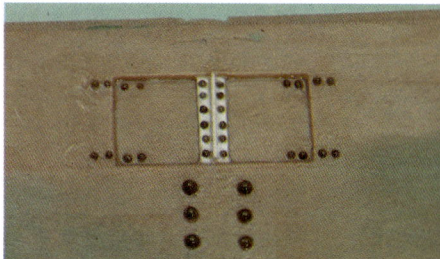

Note how the new upper 'window' requires many rivets and much reinforcement.

from plastic strip, the vehicle walls eventually being improved by incorporating gunsight covers.

The floor should be changed to not only incorporate the correct non-slip coating but the different

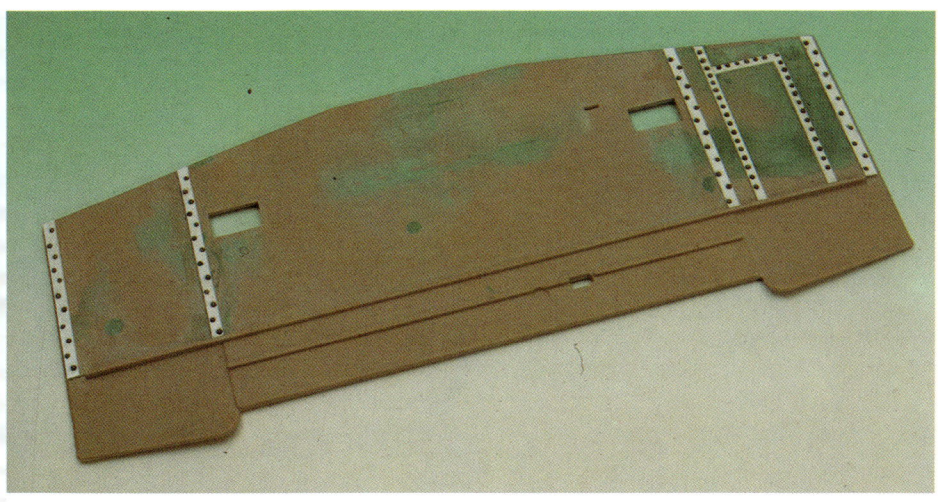

The door frame and metal joints are reinforced by plastic strip, rivets being reproduced using perforated metal sheet.

Below the embrasure a riveted reinforcement is needed to anchor the machine guns.

Hinges for the rear door need changing as they are moulded on the wrong side.

Two small sights protected by metal sheets may be added to the front armour plate.

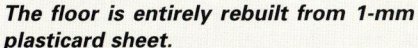

The floor is entirely rebuilt from 1-mm plasticard sheet.

sections and levels giving access to the storage areas below it. This entails drawing out each area required on 1-mm plastic sheet and cutting several pieces to make up the new floor. Non-slip strips are then glued into position. In the rear of the A7V there is an area free of equipment with a trapdoor and hatches that enable details of the vehicle's drive to be seen. The octagonal support for the 57-mm gun is built in the same way, the

A ballpoint pen is used to draw out the floor dividers.

The non-slip material for the floor is cut as required with hinges and rivets added from plastic strip and rod.

The non-slip material for the floor is cut as required with hinges and rivets added from plastic strip and rod.

The rear end of the vehicle is quite bare except for slots for the drive train and the transmission.

An octagonal piece supports the barrel of the main gun and the kit part, suitably modified, may be used. Alternatively, a new component can be made.

using a hollow length of tubing in brass or by drilling-out plastic dowel using progressively finer files. A final polish with a scouring pad and wet and dry sandpaper will produce the desired turned metal effect. Most of the remedial work to make the Tauro A7V into an impressive replica is confined to the crew compartment as the engine and transmission are hidden under the floor.

The gun is further detailed by adding the recoil cylinders and a transverse axle from plastic rod set into pre-drilled holes. The protective metal sheet for the recoil

shape required being previously drawn onto a paper template. Work with a file will improve the original kit gun and adding a base-plate in 0.5-mm plastic sheet will raise the weapon up a little. The gun barrel should be improved by

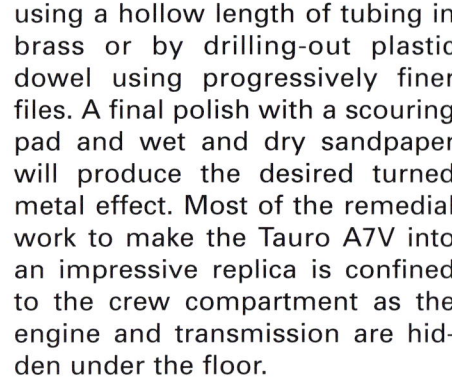

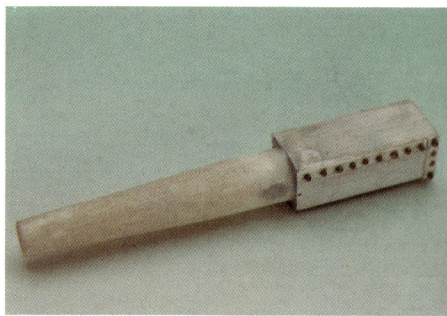

The gun barrel was completely rebuilt from tubing.

mechanism is made from thin plastic sheet and the cylinder bolts are fashioned from plastic rod, small sections of which is also used for rivets. The cylinder head is built up from 1-mm plastic sheet, rounded and formed to follow the contours of the full size item, with plastic strip sections

A view of the complete floor showing the central area where the engine and upper driving platform are located.

being added where appropriate. The breech block is built up in the same way.

Armour plate to protect the main gun must incorporate two circular sections joined together with a central opening to take the barrel as a sub-assembly for location into the gun carriage.

A small cylindrical section of tubing will be required to make the telescopic sight which is 0.5-mm diameter in this scale. Measurements for these smaller items should of course be checked against scale plans. The gun barrel area has a strengthened wall with two 0.3-mm angle iron strips.

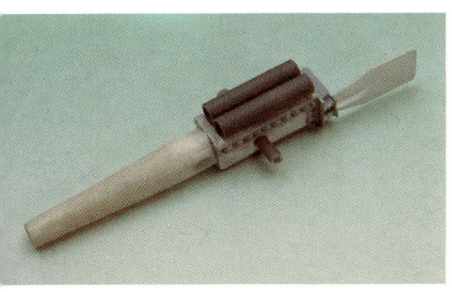

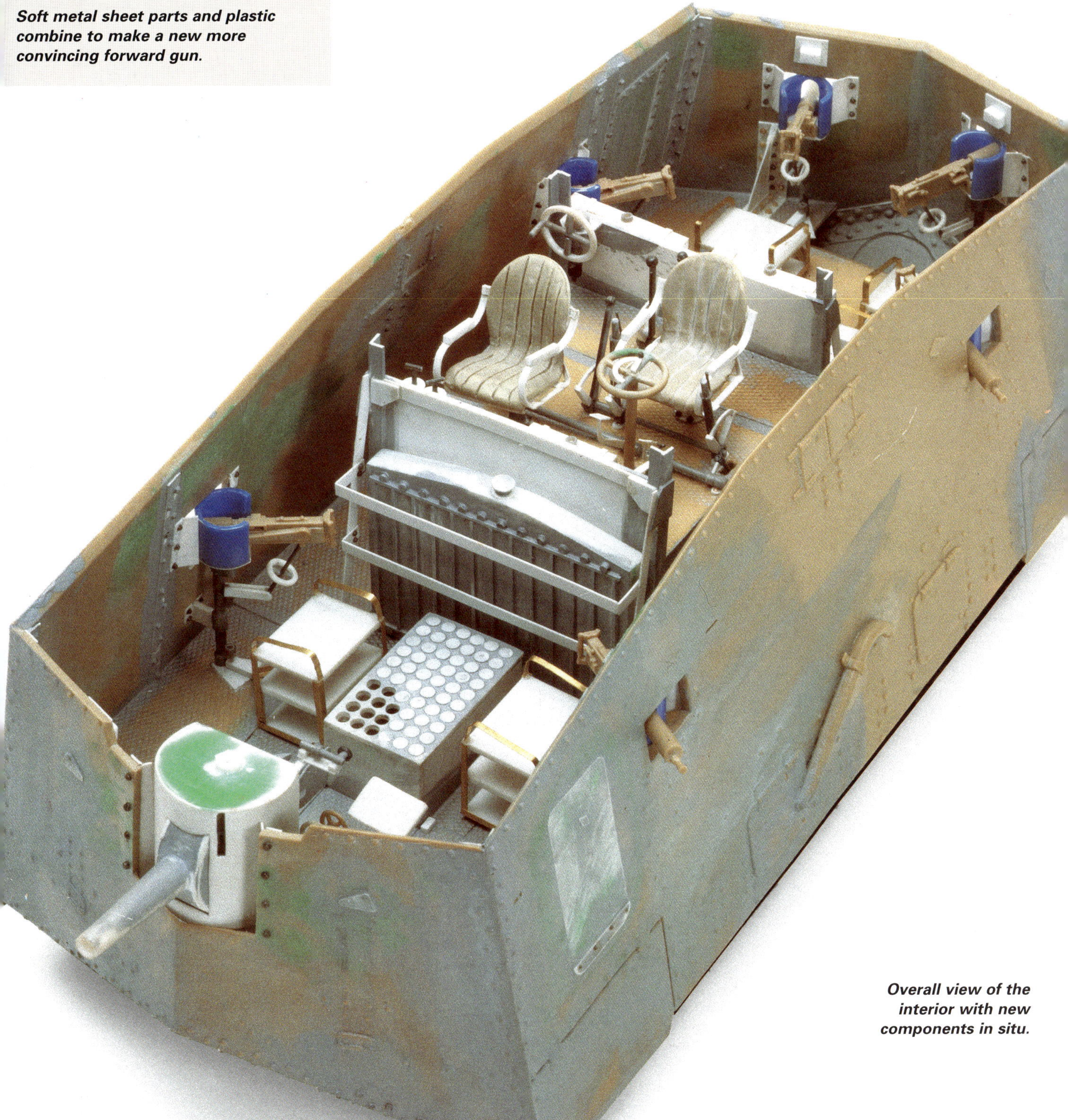

Soft metal sheet parts and plastic combine to make a new more convincing forward gun.

Overall view of the interior with new components in situ.

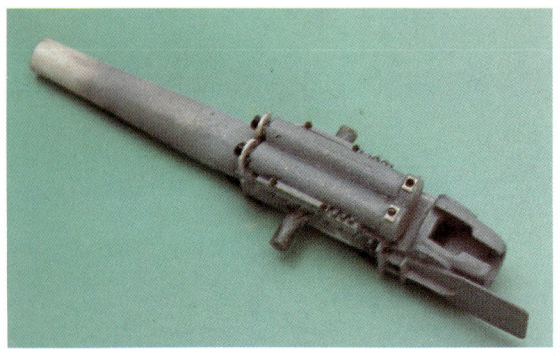

Gun breech cylinder detail and barrel protection made from plastic strip.

For the protective cover for the cylinder, a number of plastic discs are required.

Drill round holes to take the barrel and its telescopic sight.

radius arms made from plastic strip. Both control wheels are joined to the central axle and connected to the gun carriage. To make the telescopic sight, cut several pieces of 8/10-in strip and attach them to sections of tube. The completed sight is situated on the left side of the barrel.

Gun ammunition was carried in a single storage area holding sixty rounds; the box is a rectangle with six shells on the short side and ten on the long side. The box itself is constructed from 1-mm card appropriately marked out beforehand, with slots left empty to indicate that rounds have already been fired.

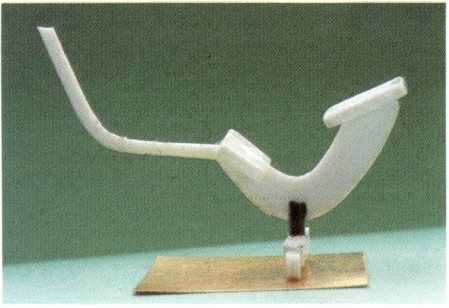

A seat and its support cut from 1-mm plastic shhet.

handwheel height adjuster. A different control wheel, one that directs the elevation and traverse movement of the gun, needs to be attached to the barrel. This control is in two sections, the larger of which can be taken from the kit while the smaller wheel is scribed with a punch and cut out with two

CREW SEATS

The A7V's main gun operator used a backless, padded seat which needs to be added to the model. After drawing on the seat dimensions, cut it from 1-mm plastic sheet and fashion it to the correct shape with file and sandpaper. Under the seat add a

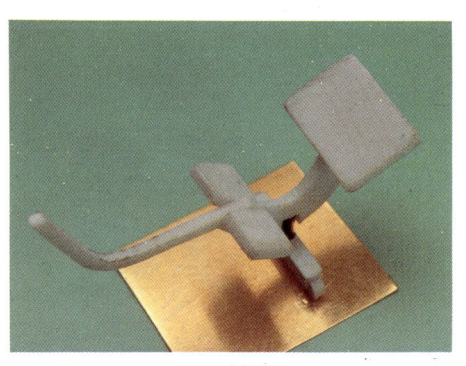

Use of a sharp knife and file enable the curved seat backs to be created.

The range-finder included in the kit can be used although a second control wheel needs to be added.

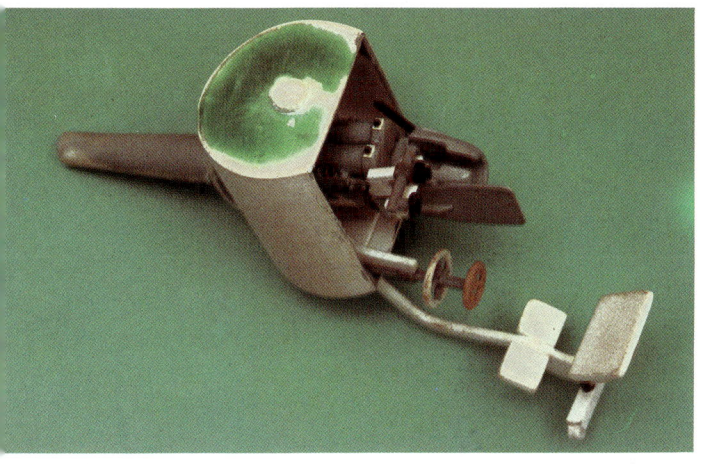

An optical sight is built from round sections of plastic strip to varying diameters.

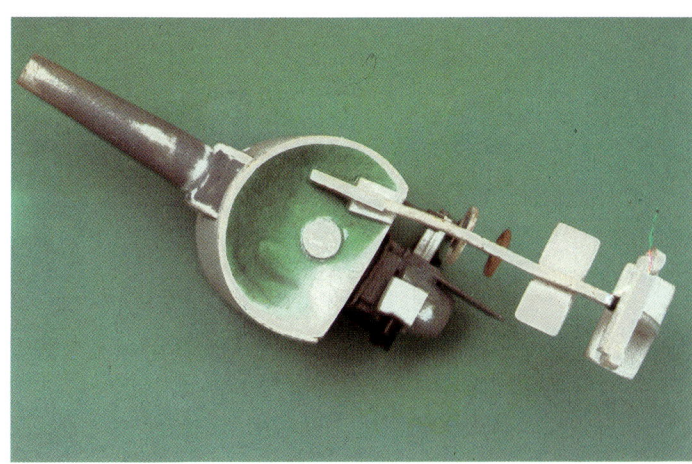

A low-angle view of the barrel showing the anchored seat and hand wheel adjusters.

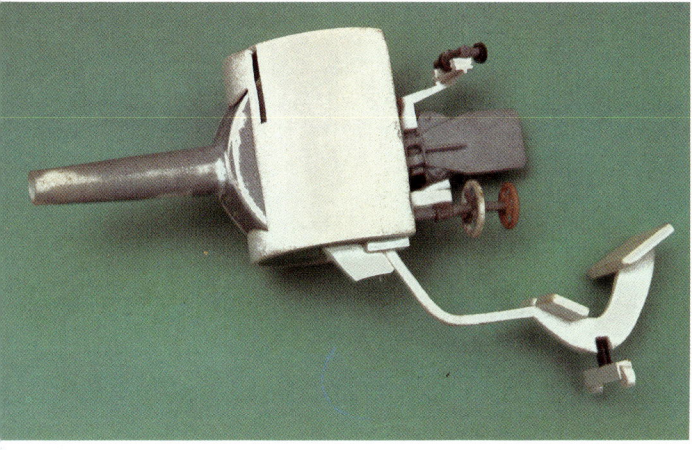

The gun barrel and its new components represent a complete sub-assembly and care is needed to make measurements correctly.

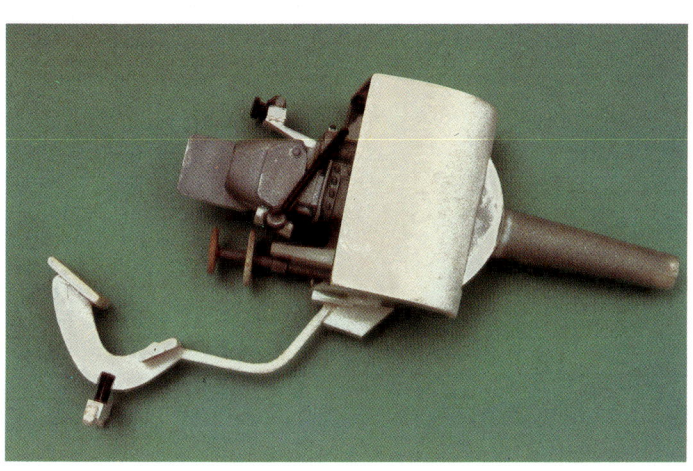

The completed assembly should turn freely.

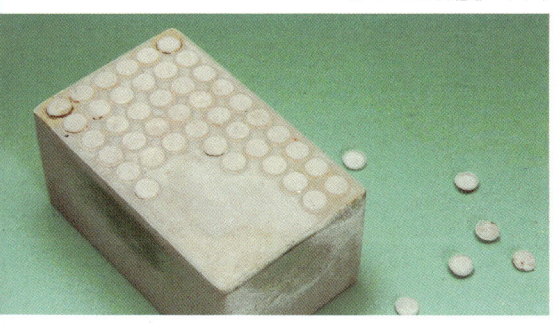

New ammunition boxes, which hold 60 rounds, are stowed on racks below each gunner's seat.

There are two types of seat for the machine gunners, the A7V having accommodation for a maximum of eighteen men. There are seven seats in this particular model with two higher ones in the forward section of the vehicle. These are in three tiers and incorporate racks for ammunition stowage underneath. Five smaller seats are set in the rear section with one in the centre. In addition, each has rudimentary 'armrests' on each side. The entire structure of all the seats may be made from 1-mm plastic sheet (for the seat base).and strips of 3/10-in brass sheet (for the supports). As it has inherent strength, brass is ideal for items such as seats which have to support weight, however small this may be: mark out and cut enough strips for all the seats being included in the kit. A support arm for each Maxim machine gun is attached to the seat base nearest the weapon, and all the guns need to have handgrips.

When it comes to the radiator, the kit parts are found to be dimensionally undersize when checked against a scale plan. Transfer the correct dimensions onto 2-mm plasticard, cut two pieces and join these to four 1-mm thick pieces. Seal the joints and sand smooth. A water intake pipe needs to be located in the upper part of the radiator, this being fashioned from a section of plastic tubing. The

Rear view of the finished vehicle. The inside distribution is different to the kit one.

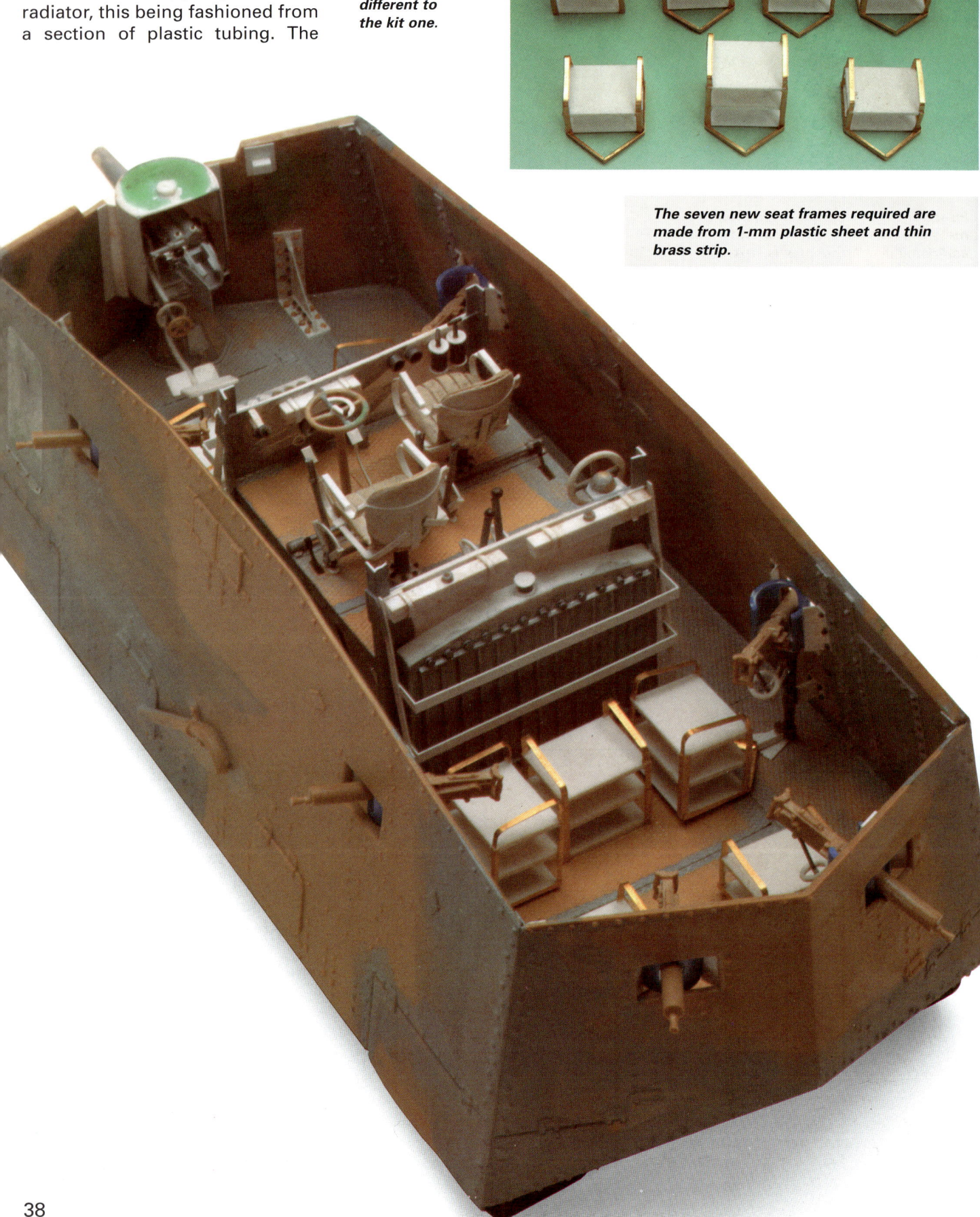

The seven new seat frames required are made from 1-mm plastic sheet and thin brass strip.

Plastic sheet 2-mm thick is required to make the new radiator, which has additional detail from plastic strip.

Draw out new oval seat backs onto plastic sheet with a ballpoint pen before cutting out.

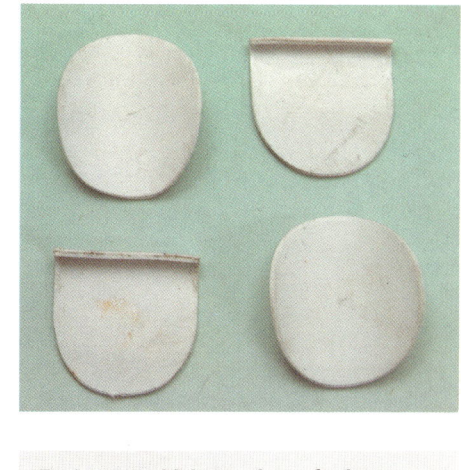

Each seat which consists of a lower section and a back, can be made from 5-mm plastic sheet.

cells of the radiator core are made from thirteen sections of thin strip, glued in position vertically and equally spaced. The top of the radiator core is held in position by twelve large nuts spaced along a bar and positioned between each vertical cell section. These can be taken from a Verlinden resin accessory kit or scratch built, again from plastic tubing.

Two seats in the centre section of the A7V are of a different type to those used by the gunners but their construction follows a similar pattern. The oval back requires two sections, one slightly smaller than the other, bent into a slight curve and glued together using an

epoxy adhesive. This results in a component strong enough to hold a coat of filler fashioned into a cushion with knife blade and abrasive. A final smoothing completes the job. The seat arms are made from plastic strip, folded

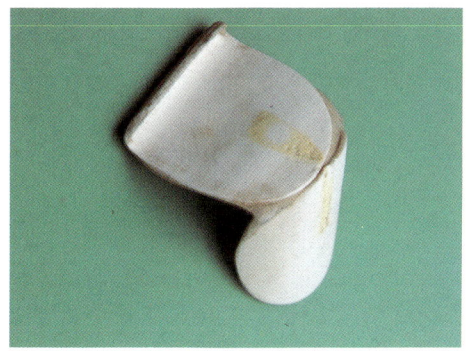

Both seat sections should be glued and given a first coat of epoxy putty.

Only a thin first coat of putty is necessary.

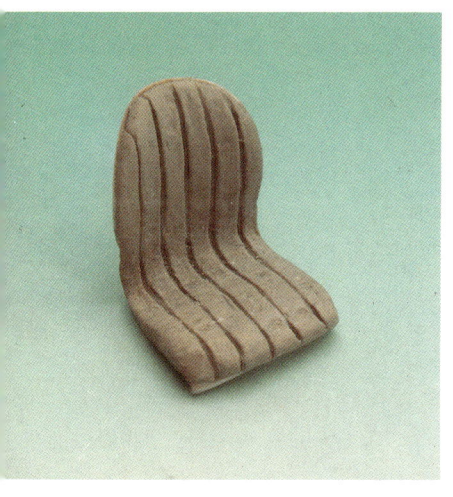

A second coat of putty gives enough thickness for indentations to be made on the simulated fabric areas.

Seat arms are made from plastic strip bent to the required shape.

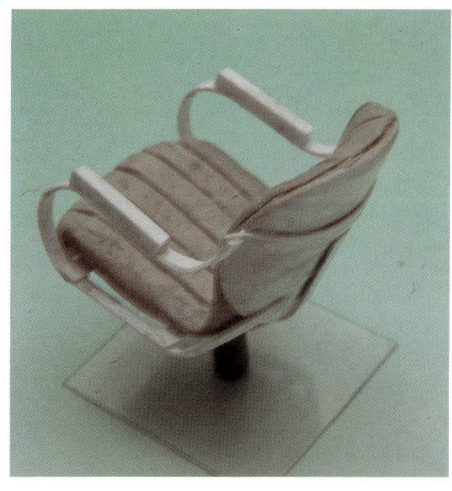

Seat cushions are formed from squares of plastic sheet and a cylindrical support is made to fix the completed seat to the floor.

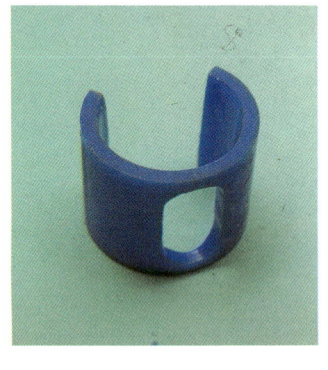

The machine gun shields are adapted from ballpoint pen handles with the kit barrels inserted.

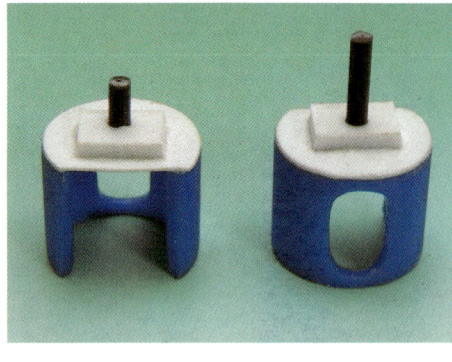

Plastic sheet provides reinforcement for the base of the shields.

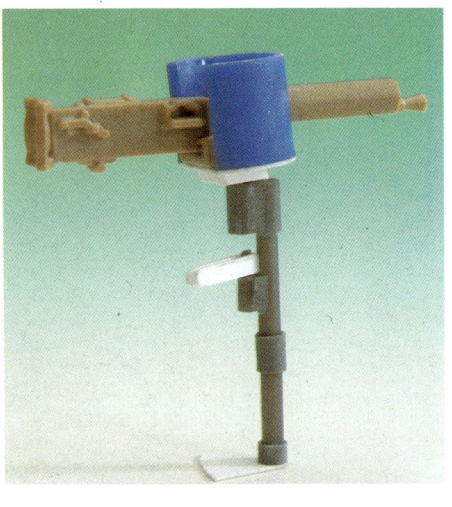

Each machine gun pintel is attached to the wall of the vehicle.

Two upper supports are needed for the pintels on which the Maxims are mounted.

and shaped to follow the original seat design with pieces added to make up the support. Seat cushions are made, like the others, from shaped putty. Finally, each seat is attached to a plastic tube riser and set on a circular base which had prominent rivets anchoring it to the floor.

Sections of hollow ballpoint pen handle make an ideal set of barrel jackets, one for each Maxim machine gun. Each base is cut from plastic sheet and strip, as are the pintels that support the guns. These pintels are strengthened by

Between the front armoured shield and the wall are two sheet metal covers.

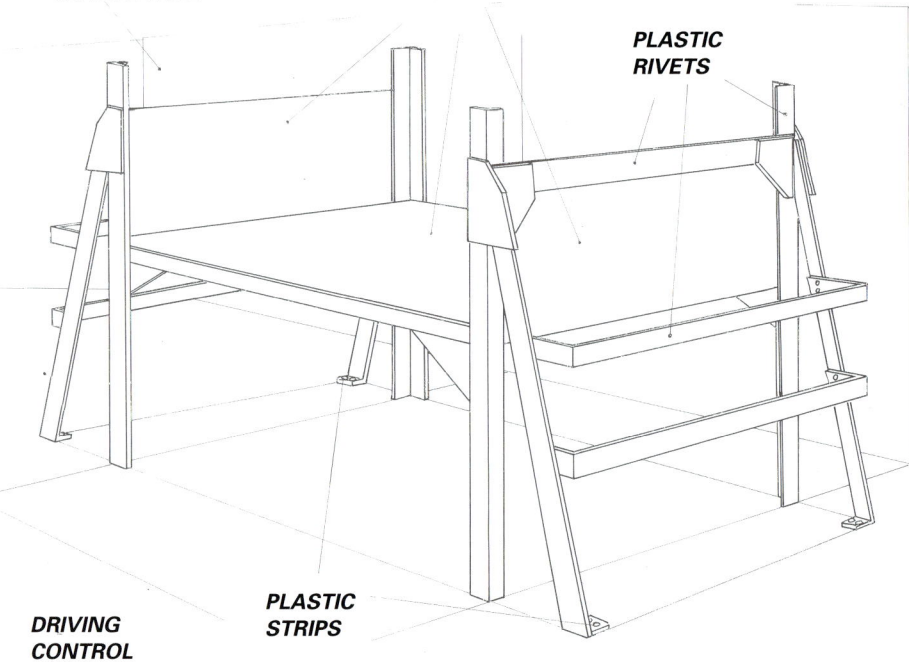

VEHICLE HULL

0.3-MM PLASTICARD

PLASTIC RIVETS

DRIVING CONTROL PLATFORM

PLASTIC STRIPS

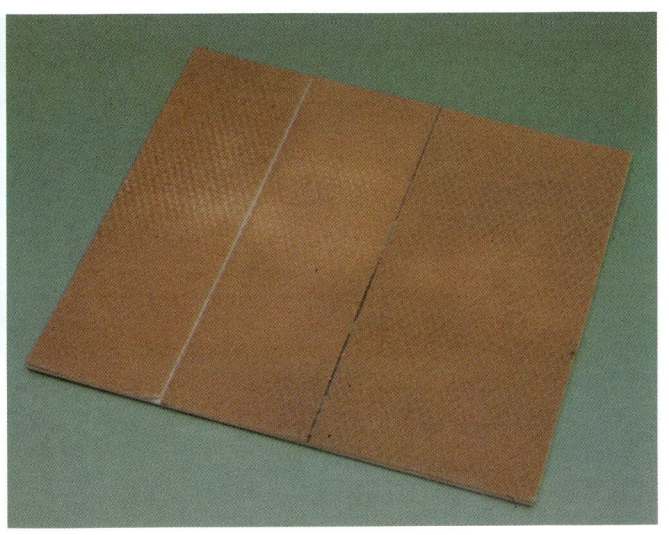

The raised driving platform has three flooring sections with a non-slip coating. This hides most of the engine and transmission.

supports riveted to the wall of the vehicle - which means further work for the ever-useful plastic sheet. Adding the two-part control wheel that alters the elevation of the gun adds to the realistic effect in this area of the model.

What might be termed the 'driving platform' is situated over the engine compartment and comprises a framework with reinforcement strips joined and riveted by corner sections and covered with non-slip flooring. Made out of 1-mm plastic sheet, this area needs to have a number of cut outs to take the control rods for the engine, drive levers and brake pedals. Rods and pedals, constructed from plastic

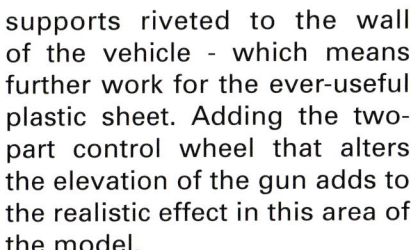

Positioning of some new components will need dexterity!

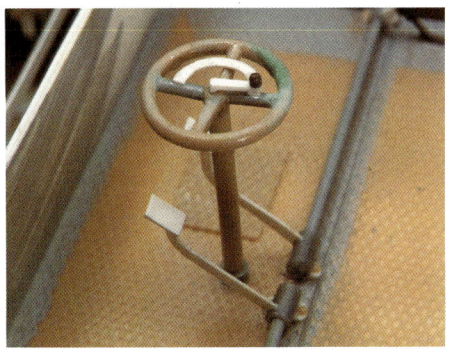

To improve the look of the driving position, give the steering wheel four spokes and add the footpedals.

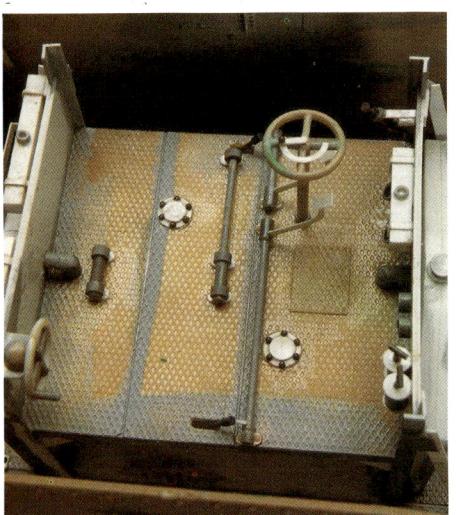

A view of the model's floor area shows the drive train and seat locations.

A secondary control wheel with spokes cut from plastic strip needs to be located aft of the driving position.

Up front, plastic tubing and strip is used for the various additional items of equipment.

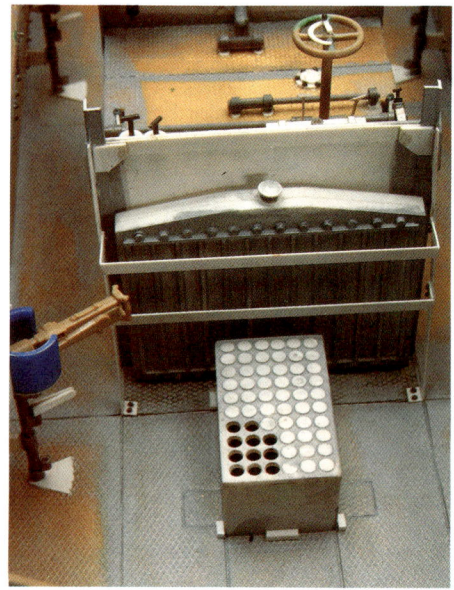

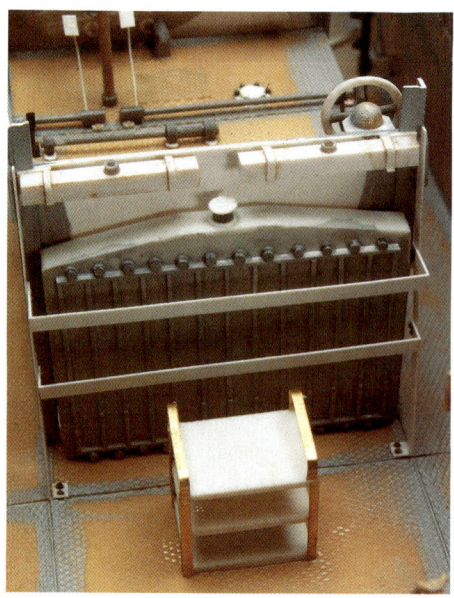

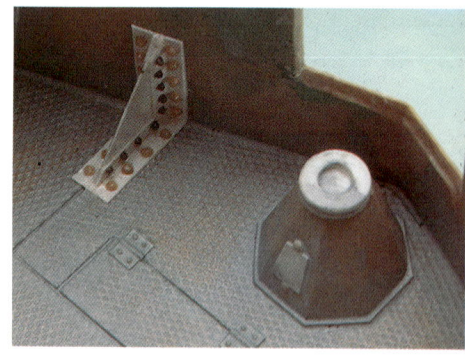

The new ammunition box is located forward of the radiator.

Plastic strip is added to the rear of the radiator.

The pedestal mounting for the gunner's seat.

strip using a combination of different sizes where necessary, need additional small location plates attached to the floor. Slots can be cut to show the limit of fore and aft travel of each lever.

Tubing, square section strip and plastic sheet combine to create the dials set into the front and rear walls of the A7V, the main control wheel coming from the kit components. This is situated in front of the seat in an horizontal position with four spokes instad of the six indicated in the kit. Simply remove all of these, discard two and reposition the spokes in the correct pattern. An auxiliary control wheel set into the rear wall has to be scratch built from 1-mm plastic. Cut it out with a compass and sand the edges to rounded section, not forgetting to add the spokes from plastic strip.

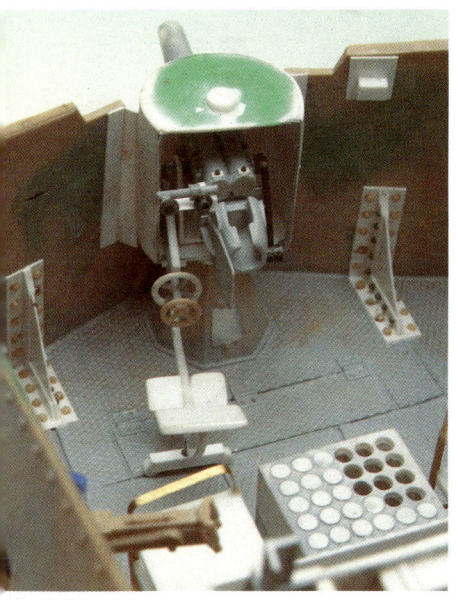

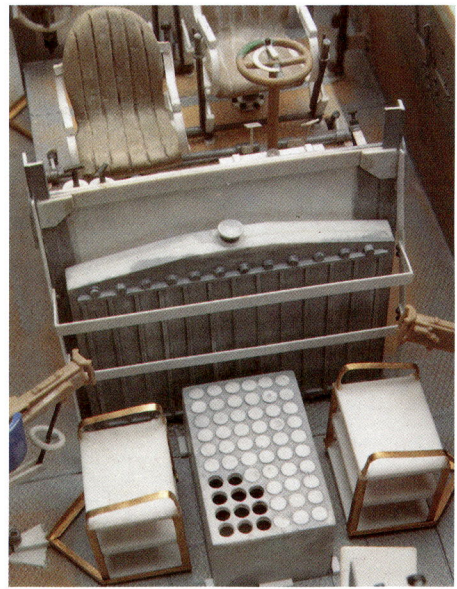

It is important to position the gun barrel correctly and add a pivot which fixes it to the base.

The centre seats for the gunners are joined to the supporting base.

The rear seats and machine guns. Each weapon has a control wheel for elevation and depression.

When all the new component parts are positioned on the driving platform, the difference is very noticable compared to the basic look of the original kit. The add-itions make for both interest and authenticity.

Final touches include adding plastic washers above and below the gun breech, setting the angle of the barrel and completing the armour plate by adding extra rivets and reinforcement strips.

The structure of the A7V reflects the fact that it was Germany's first attempt to develop a practical tank; rather than to totally enclose the crew in an armoured box, it resembled a bathtub on caterpillar tracks - but for kit display purposes the 'open top' configuration does allow the extra detail to readily be seen. If the exhaust shields and additional protection provided for the driver are left off, almost all the detail can be checked at a glance. As with any model project involving making and positioning small parts, considerable patience and a methodical approach to the work is required. The foregoing descrip-tion covers most of what is needed and the new components are in themselves, relatively simple to construct.

COMPLEMENTARY ITEMS

Despite its light armament the A7V carried a considerable amount of ammunition, boxed in much the same way as that used by the MG-34 or -42 machine guns fitted to World War II vehicles. Extra rounds found in Tamiya injection moulded kits, Verlinden resin AFV accessories or Andrea Miniatures components which are cast in lead, can be used with this WWI tank. Spare ammunition belts stowed under the seats or in various racks, add to that 'ope-rational' look.

VEHICLE EXTERIOR

Few changes have been sug-gested on the outside of this kit because the supplied components require little modification apart from the removal of some panels which are the wrong size. Some work also needs to be done to pro-vide the correct number of hatches in their right locations.

The steering column with control levers grouped around the seats.

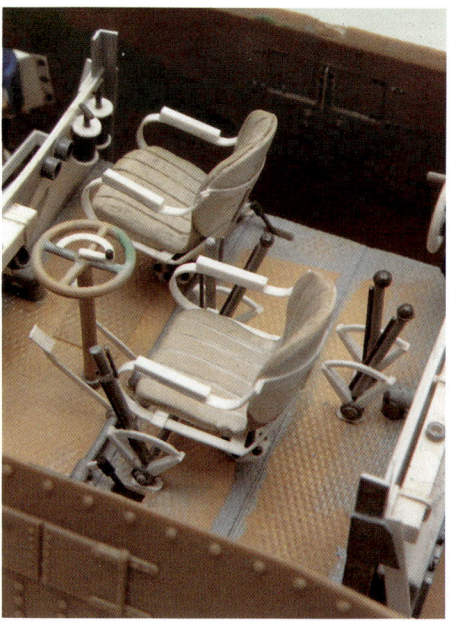

The finished driving position with new instruments and controls.

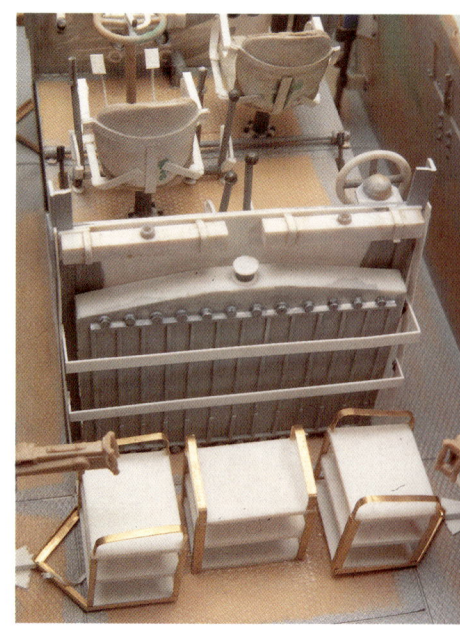

Locate one of the rear seats in the centre and the other adjacent to the machine gun positions.

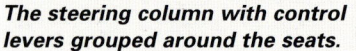

Perforated hatches protect the gunners while a central cover shields the driving position from small arms fire.

SCRATCH BUILT TANK TRANSPORTER

Having described the building of commercial
kits and carrying out some conversion
work to make different variants, the ultimate project is
to build a vehicle totally from scratch.
Acquired skills of this kind will
enable the keen modeller to add virtually any AFV to
his collection.

STAGES OF SCRATCH BUILDING

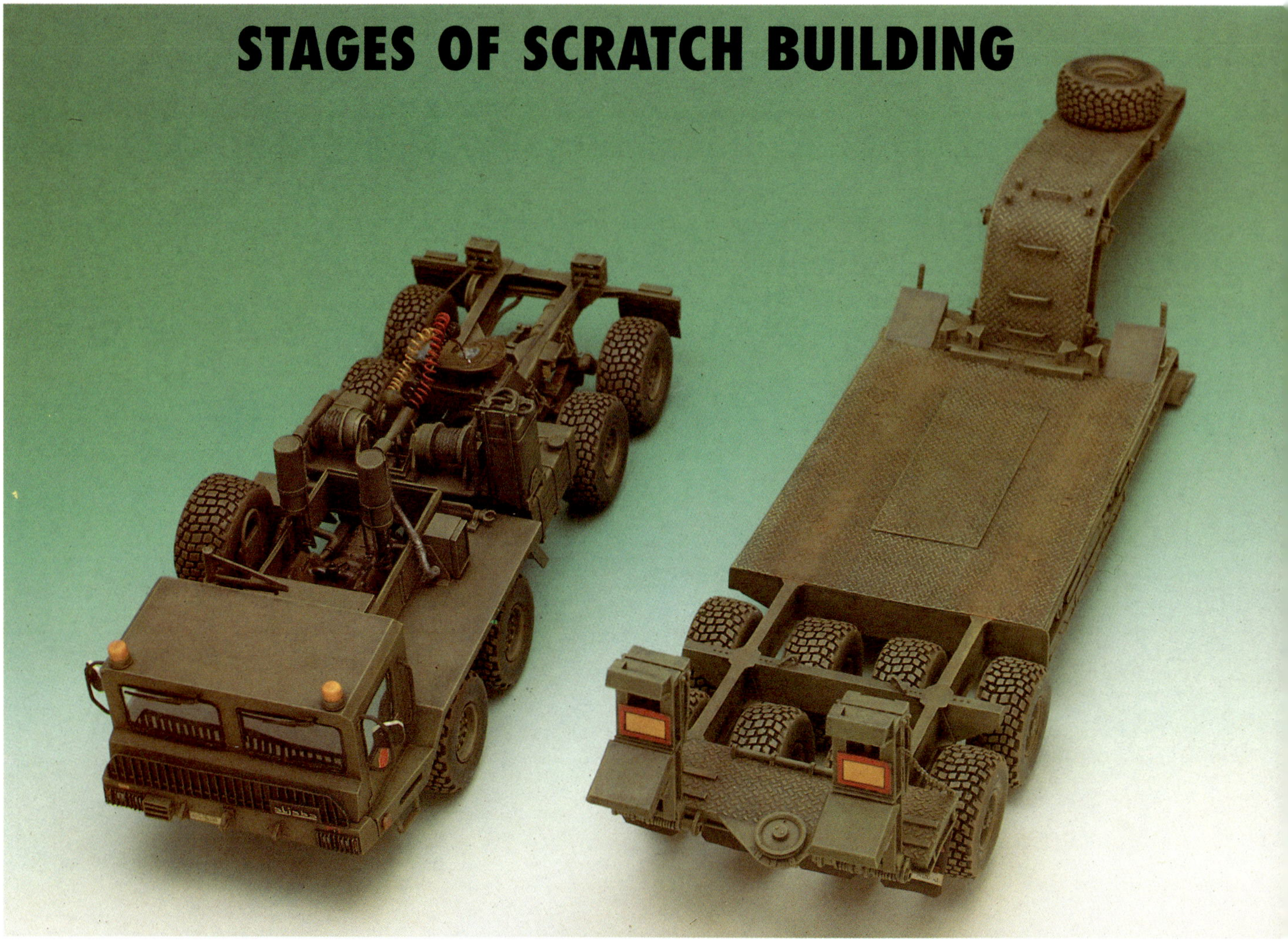

When you have decided which vehicle to build there are some important points to consider:

Are the necessary references to hand or if not, can these be acquired?

Can you plan the project well in terms of time so that the work does not become frustrating?

Is a full range of materials adaptable to modelling available?

Check if you have enough of the right tools and obtain new scalpel blades, sandpaper and so forth; a surprisingly large range of hand and power tools can be used in a scratch-build modelling programme.

Our project was greatly aided by photographs of the full size vehicle and such material should be added to the printed references

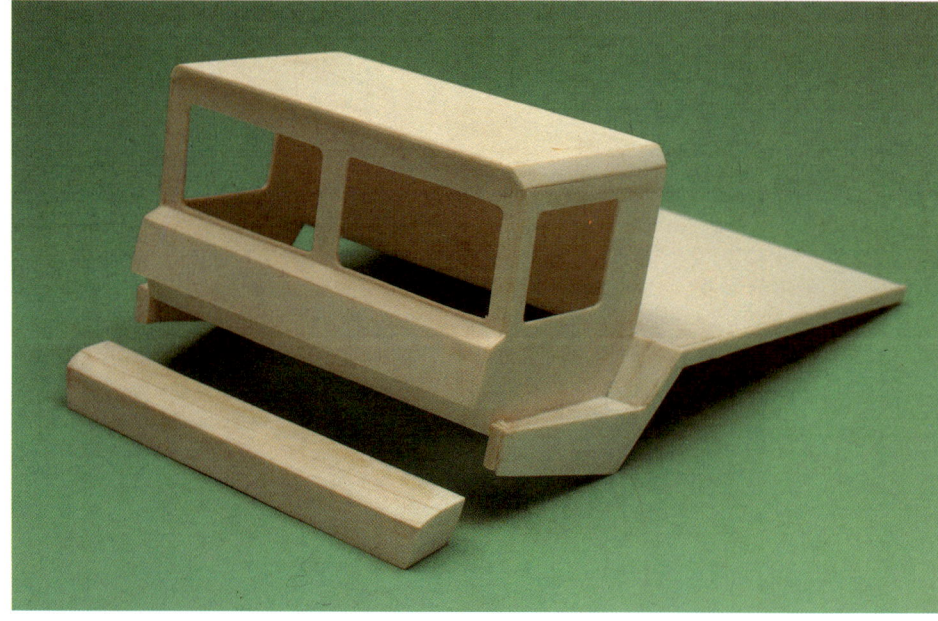

The cab has several pieces which are measured out, cut to size and glued into position.

that will form the basis of the model.

Firstly the cab and prime mover section are to be built followed by the trailer with its transporter section, the main purpose of this vehicle. The different thicknesses of plasticard required are: 0.25-mm, 0.50-mm, 1-mm, 1.5-mm and 2-mm. Flat plastic strip in various widths is also very useful.

Plastic strip		Manufacturer's Ref No
1/4 x 1/4	12 x 12 mm	199 B
3/16 x 3/16	9 x 9 mm	196 B
	0.3 x 0.3 mm	131 B
	5 x 9 mm	178 B
	5 x 5 mm	175 B
	0.2 x 0.2 mm	120 B
	0.1 x 0.2 mm	100 B

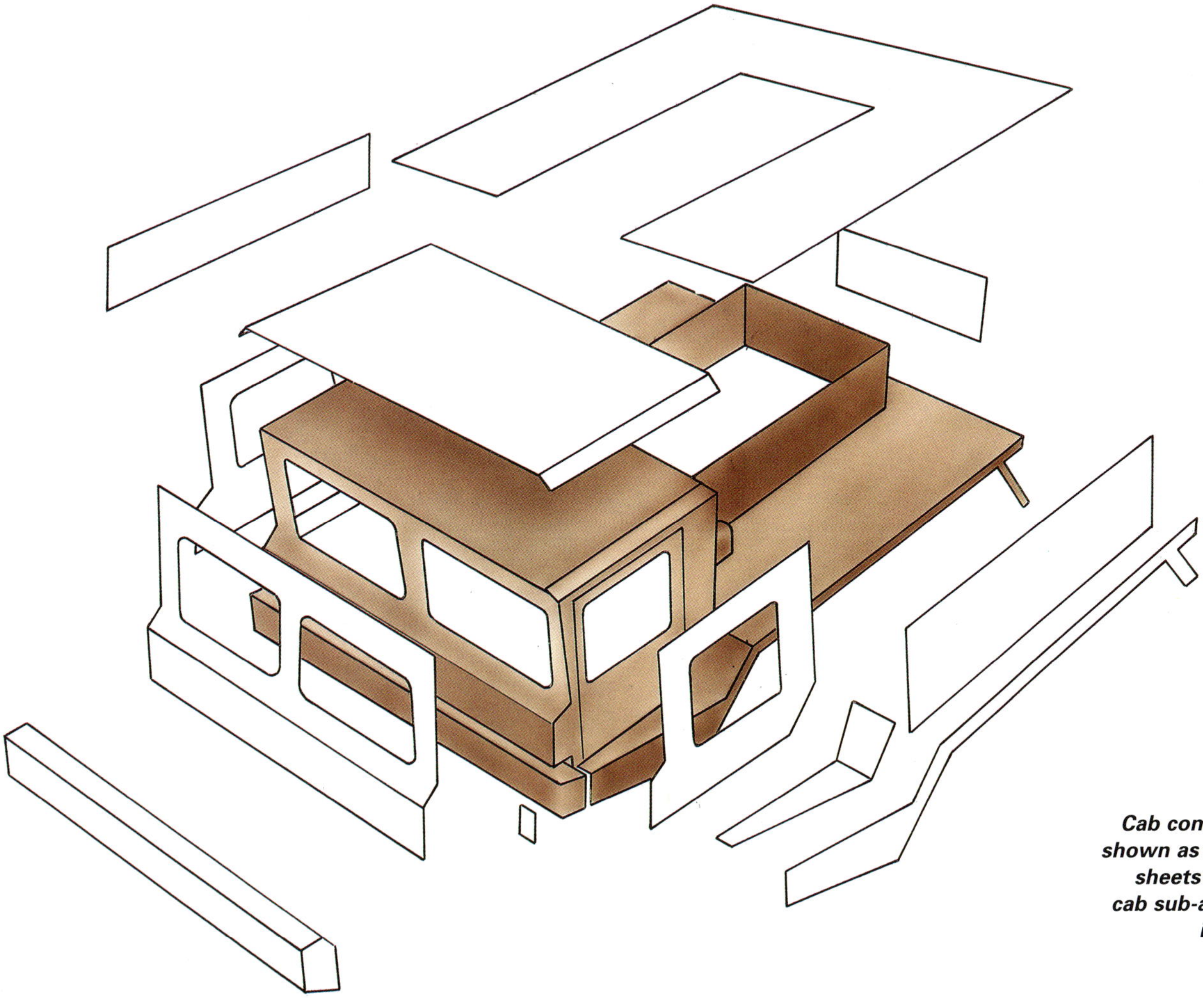

The seats, steering wheel and some controls are taken from a similar kit in the same scale. New sections are cut from plasticard.

Cab components shown as separate sheets with the cab sub-assembly in colour.

In addition, plastic tubing in the following diameters will be very useful: 3.2-mm; 1.5-mm, 1.7-mm, 2.3-mm and 2-mm. Non slip coating for flooring is obtainable from photoetch sets. Synthetic resin is used to make the tyres and copper wire in various thicknesses lends itself well to reproducing the electrical and hydraulic pipes and hoses in the prime mover.

Chains sold for use with marine models in 15-cm width are used, as are perforated plastic strips.

BUILDING THE CHASSIS

The lower area of this massive road-going vehicle consists of an immensely strong chassis formed from a series of strong box sections with reinforced cross members. To make the model a start is made by constructing the forward chassis section which supports the driving cab and engine section of the vehicle. The necessary flat 'U' section piece for the framework might be obtainable commercially

although we opted to build it. Start by glueing two thin strips of plastic sheet to two longer ones which will eventually be positioned along each edge of the chassis. Repeat this stage to complete the 'U' section framework.

The inside chassis crossbeams and smaller items to complete the sub-assembly are glued together. Measure the area occupied by the leaf springs and construct these from a sandwich of 1-mm wide plastic strips set at a 90 degree angle. Onto the centre of each spring set glue five pieces of plastic strip for the trailing arm suspension links. Four octagonal nuts, two for each side, are from Verlinden accessories.

When you have built the entire framework and added the pieces that support the wheel sets, these should be put to one side rather than glued because a width check will be necessary before final assembly. The logical next step is to make the two box sections enclosing the four axles and leaf springs. It is worth checking the spares box

for these items as some 1/24 scale commercial vehicle models have similar components that can be adapted to our transporter project. Similar but unfortunately not identical parts are to be found in some truck kits manufactured by Ertl, notably the IH 5000 Paystar. Two kits will be have to be obtained for them to yield sufficient parts. Comparing these parts with our plans if is found that:

(1) the length and height of the leaf springs needs to be increased

(2) the crossmember that joins the axles should be of equal length on both sides

(3) only the centre of the Ertl kit axles can be used as these are round and ours need to be of square section.

Modification is as follows: to heighten the leaf springs, cut the kit items at the joint of the trapezium piece that supports the cross member between the axles and add a 0.5-mm piece of plasticard. To lengthen the springs add a 0.5-mm piece at both ends of the upper leaf.

48

Shorten the join between the axles by trimming 2.5-mm off each side. Cut with a saw and form with a file before glueing.

To modify the axle bars slim them down with a file and add four 0.5-mm sections of plasticard at both ends.

The assemblies comprising the wheels and axles are now finished apart from adding the four hexagonal nuts from a Verlinden accessory kit. The upper set of nuts is attached to a 3-mm diameter plasticard disc. Follow scale plans of the vehicle to ascertain the exact location of any new parts that have been made.

MAKING THE TYRES

Making wheels can be time consuming but there is no choice

Copper wire was utilised to make cables and hawsers, wound around their winches.

The prime mover fully assembled. The extensive use of plastic sheet in this scratch build project can be readily appreciated.

if spare ones of the correct size cannot be found in other kits. To scratch build the wheels for this kit, start with two plastic discs 2-mm thick and 40-mm wide. These provide the inner and outer hubs, with a plastic strip wound around in between them to make the tread. To attach the wheels, drill the centre of the disc to take the axle and clean up with a file and sandpaper. Lastly, enlarge the hole to accept the axle support and prepare to make the hubcaps. To reproduce the tyre tread pattern correctly, catalogues from manufacturers of tyres intended for real

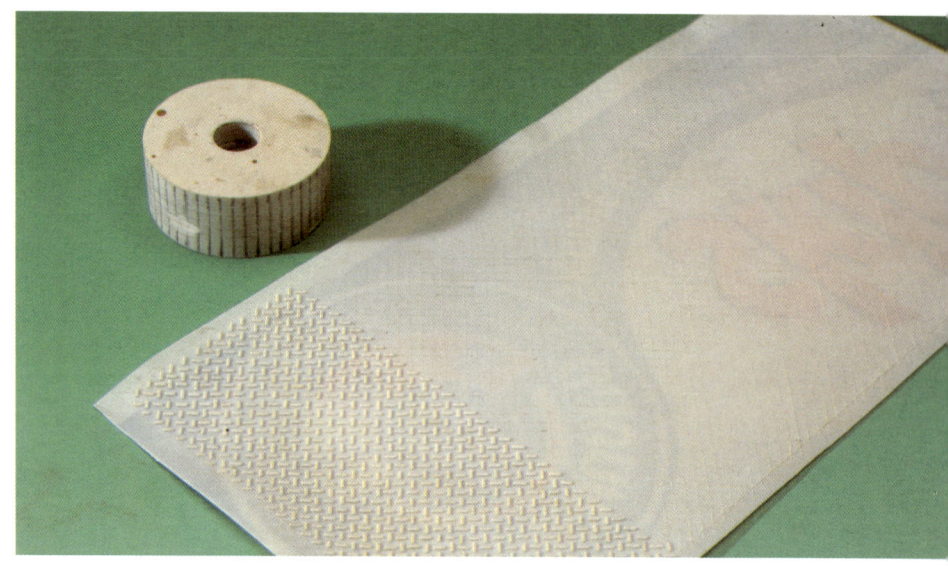

Two 2-mm thick discs are the basic elements needed to make new wheels.

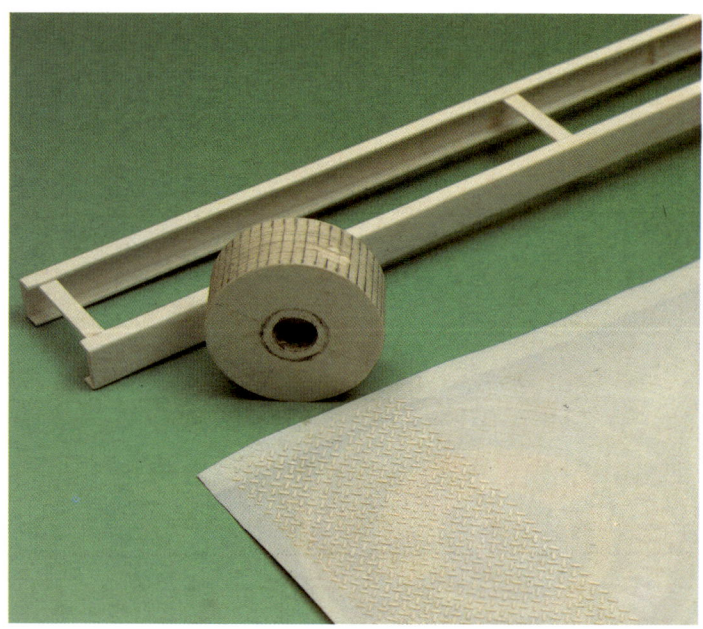

The trailer base nearing completion with supporting crossbeams and non-slip flooring made from plasticard.

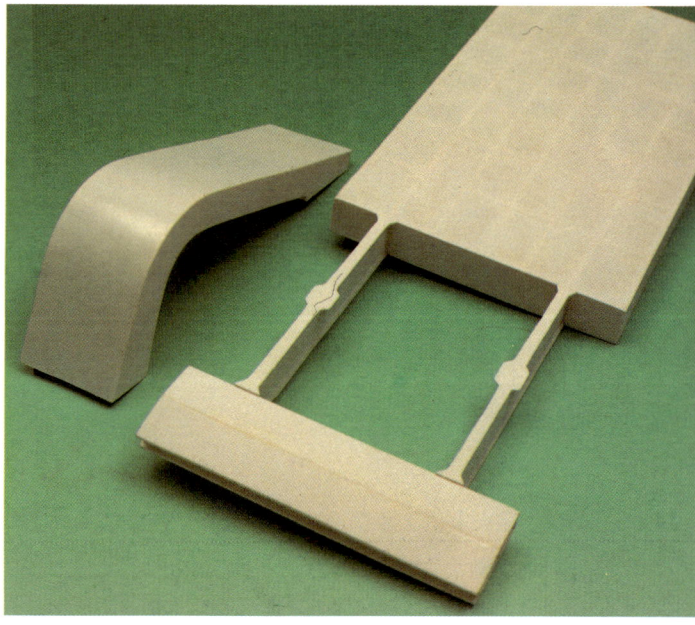

Tyre treads are made from paper templates attached to a plastic base before sanding down.

vehicles come in very handy as these form a basis for the model tyres. Xerox a photograph of a real tyre and scale it to 1/35 to fit a wheel on the model. Fix the copied tread image firmly to a plastic sheet formed into a disc wide enough for a wheel. With a very sharp knife blade, cut around the tread pattern and in effect 'print' the entire plastic disc. Clean up the

cylinder with a rag soaked in alcohol and finish by rounding off each tyre edge with a file and sandpaper.

GETTING THE FORM

When proceeding to fitting the wheels to the cab chassis it will be noticed that the hubcabs are dif-

ferent to those on the trailer wheels. To make the front wheel hubcaps, cut a 2-mm plastic disc and a tubular section 13-mm in diameter for the backplate. This needs to have eight equidistant holes each 2.7-mm across

The holes must be neat as they are the ones that take the wheel nuts; ten 3-mm Verlinden accessory kit nuts are needed and the hubcaps for this section of the vehicle are complete.

To make the hubcaps on the trailer wheels, start with a 13.8-mm diameter circle and a second one 1-mm thick. Cut out a further circle 8-mm in diameter and 0.5-mm thick. Eight 2-mm nuts, again from Verlinden, are needed for these wheels; repeat the process for the rest of the wheels.

As this vehicle has eighteen tyres including the spares, a mould that will take polyurethane resin and can be re-used, is strongly advised. Having moulded all the tyres needed the framework can be assembled together with the axles and their supports and the wheels can be placed on their axles. You should now have a chassis set ready for mating with the engine, driveshafts, mudguards and the links to the prime mover.

BUILDING THE CAB

To construct the cab of the vehicle take measurements from scale plans then cut out the various body panels. Remember to cut out the window glass area from those sections that make up the windscreen frame and the side windows. Make the cab as a box structure, adding the roof last. Some reinforcement using 1-mm plastic strip may be

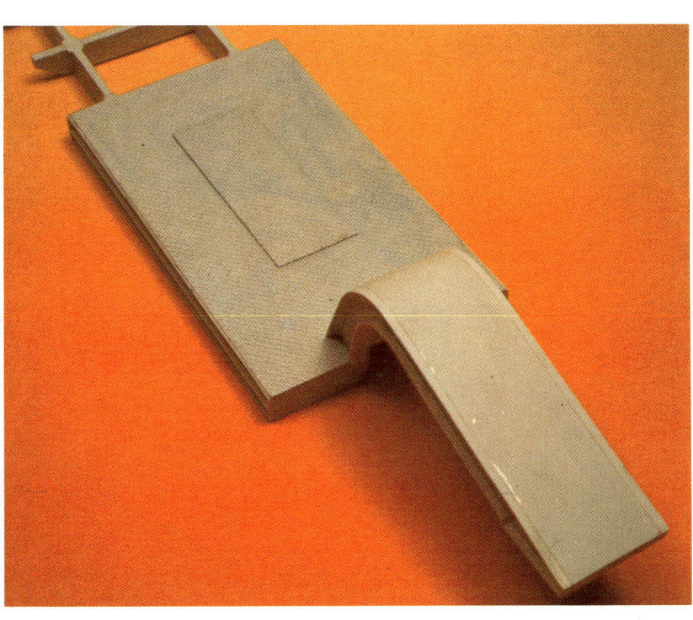

Applying large areas of non-slip covering can be simplified by using photoetch parts from accessory kits.

The lower part of the trailer ramp showing how the cross members are made to support the curved sections .

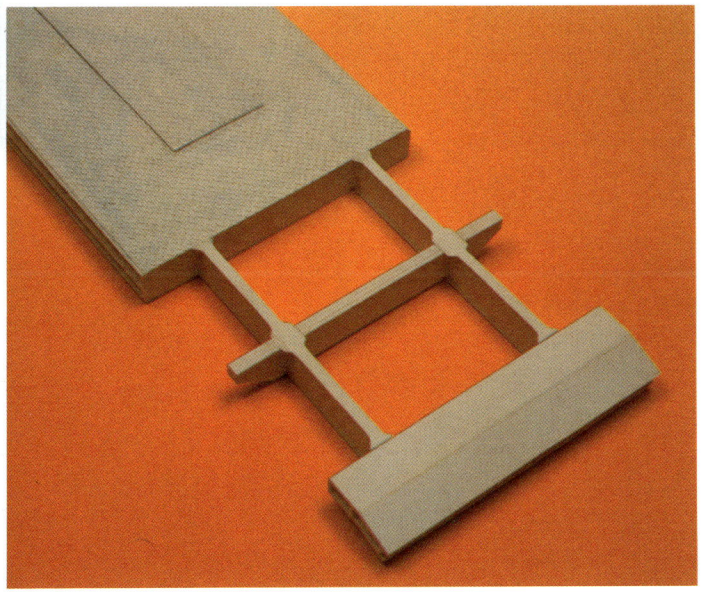

Crossbeams are formed by three 1-mm thick sections with a 0.5-mm thick covering, glued and trimmed to fit.

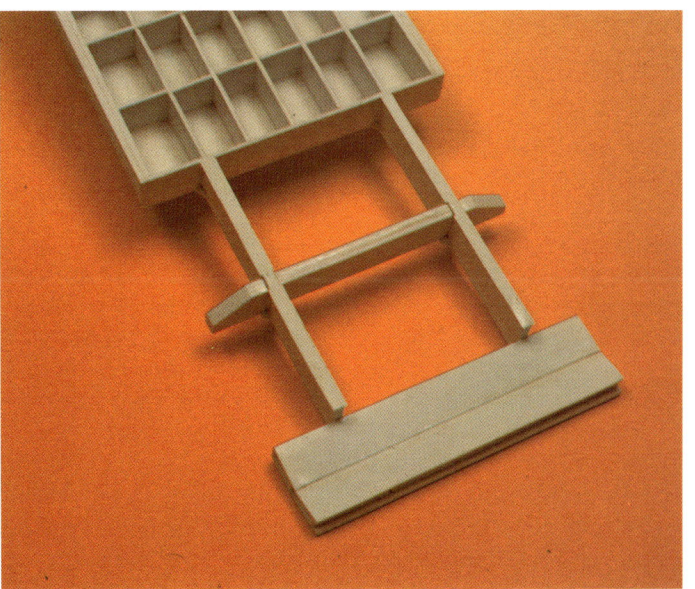

Reinforcement of the lower trailer is achieved by adding 1-mm or 2-mm plastic strip.

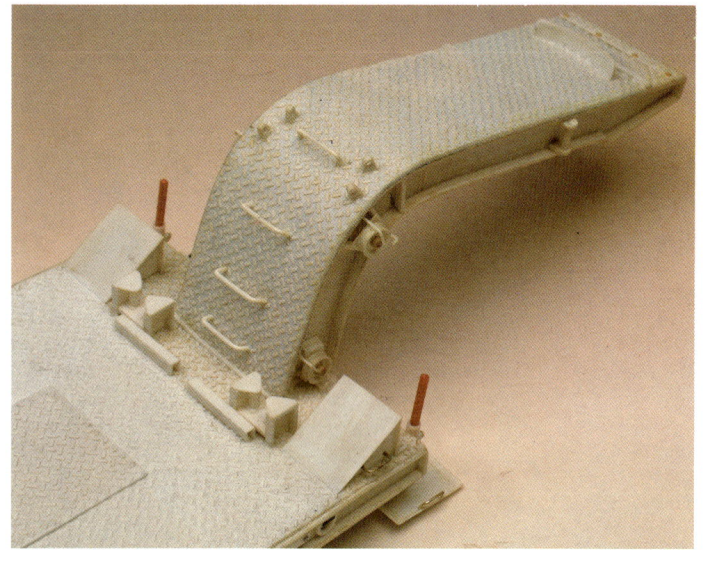

General view of the trailer bridge with added details including cable guides, floor stops and ladder, all made out of plasticard.

All the wheels and their double axle collars can be duplicated from a single original.

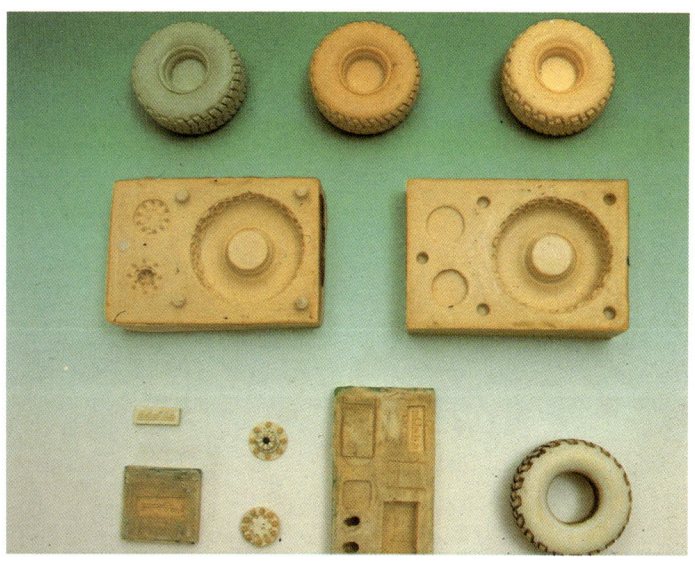

The male-female wheel mould before the resin is poured. The mould is joined only when the resin compound has set.

The axle supports are quite complex, requiring as they do nine separate components shaped from 2-mm thick plastic sheet and 40-mm diameter discs. Holes made with a mini-drill need careful finishing with a file and sandpaper.

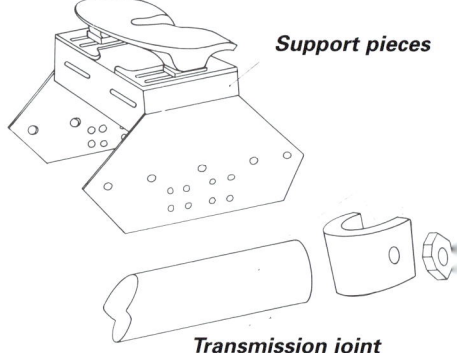

Support pieces

Transmission joint

necessary for a good rigid structure.

EXHAUSTS

A second box bay is required in which to mount the engine. The exhausts are rectangular double units, one section fitting inside the other. Make the outer one from 2-mm material, the inner one from 1-mm. Both are perforated - and be prepared to make forty slots in each one. This task is made easier by drawing vertical and horizontal lines with a fine pen. Where the lines cross, drill out using a fine, 1.2-mm drill. Each section completed can serve as a pattern for the next one needed. This area is all but finished by the spare wheel support and trailer bar located at the rear end of the cab. The support is made from 3-mm plasticard by drawing a circle with an outside diameter the same as that of a tyre, onto paper. Cut this template out and trace around it onto plastic sheet. The trailer bar is made

from 2-mm tubing. The coupling connections are two rectangular pieces which will need final shaping with files. When both these items have been completed they can be glued to the cab rear.

DIFFERENTIAL, ENGINE AND DRIVETRAIN

Luckily the entire engine block does not have to be scratch built. As a basis we used the unit from the Ertl 5000 Paystar truck kit. This will need an additional turbocharger made out of lengths of rod

The double wheels positioned in the rear section of the trailer. Before this stage, all the tyres should be sanded to remove any surplus resin.

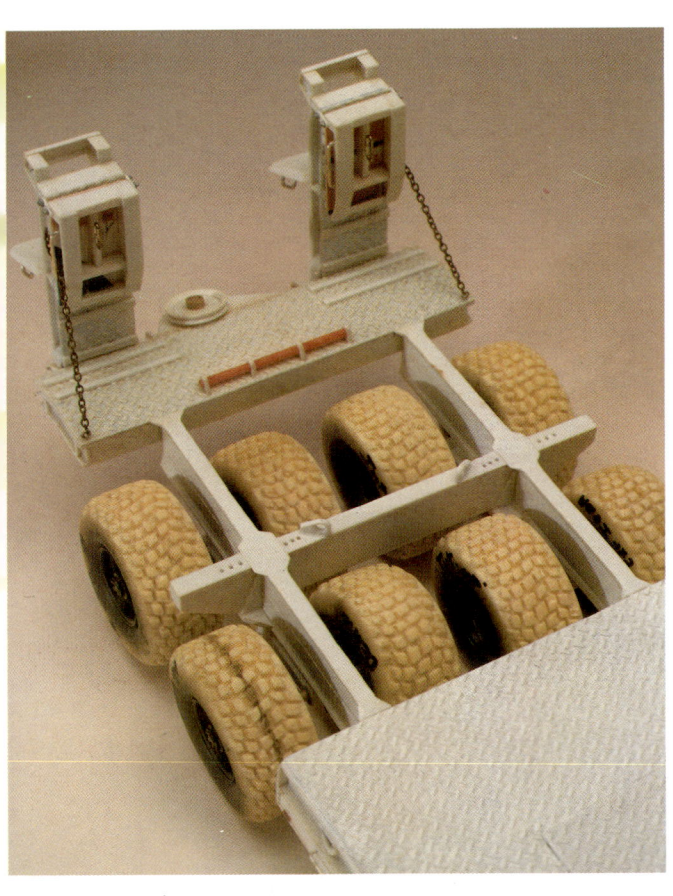

and 2-mm diameter tubing. Tubing will also come in useful for connectors.

The driveshaft needs completely rebuilding. Photographs of the full size engine will be very useful for this stage of construction but the basis here is a 20-mm long section of tubing 4-mm in diameter. This needs filing to semi-oval section.

Both axles are prepared from round 4-mm strip joined by a semi-circular plastic piece. Cut two 6-mm diameter circles and drill them out using a 3.5-mm drill. Cut each set in half and make a total of eight sections.

TRAILER SUPPORTS

When the engine and transmission are assembled and ready for joining to the rear section of the vehicle, 1-mm plasticard pieces

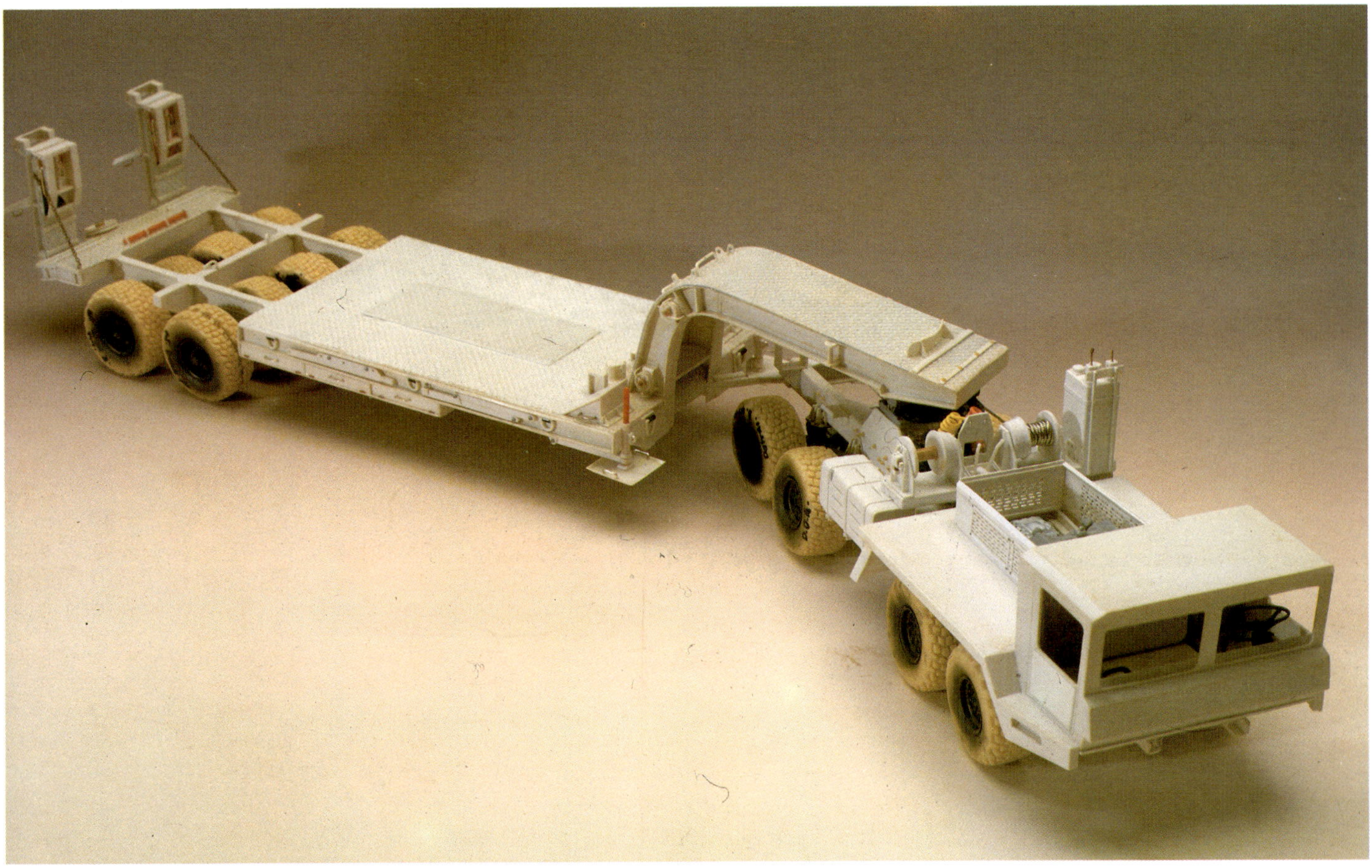

Once assembled the transporter makes a very impressive model. Build time for this example was one year, representing many manhours of work.

Roof warning beacons and the front bumper are made from plastic strip.

The unusual shape of the driver's door, which is divided horizontally.

Box-like cooling covers with ventilation grilles can be situated over the engine. The holes can be made with a drill.

The electrical connectors are made by wire wrapped around the handle of a needle file.

One of the side fuel tanks and control box for the winches.

The engine behind the cab is often left uncovered to assist cooling and ease servicing.

need to be prepared as a driveshaft support. Again, consult plans to determine the exact dimensions. The two sections of the support will be attached to the cross-members but before doing that mark out the locations for the retaining nuts. Two 6-mm wide plasticard strips and a single 1-mm wide strip encase the shaft, which is finished off by utilising the support piece from the Ertl kit. Make the rectangular fuel tanks and their supports, a job that should be straightforward enough if plans and photographs are followed closely. Trace out the reinforced tank retainers, utilising two plastic strips for each one. The tank plug and fillers are made by glueing on

The winches, guides and all other fittings have to be scratch built.

Each wheel group is attached to leaf springs fixed on the chassis.

To provide strength to the trailer attachment collar, resin screws can be used.

Overview of the prime mover area shows to advantage the front end of the transporter and the arrangement of the exhaust pipes and horn-like silencers.

three equal plastic strips as seats for one 5-mm diameter disc and one 1-mm disc.

CONSTRUCTING WINCHES

The platform that supports the electric winches and the box section guards that protect them are also made from 1-mm plasticard,

Some complexity is apparent in the curved trailer link where strong joints are essential.

A spare wheel located on top of the link arm, seen here joined to the prime mover.

with reference to the vehicle plans. The round winch bodies are built up from different diameter circular pieces of card stuck together in a conical shape. This conical sandwich can be formed and covered with putty making a firm basis for the opening slots. Plans of the full size vehicle will show that supports are also needed at this stage.

Details such as these can be added by utilising different lengths of plastic strip and rod. The steel cable supports are made up from 1-mm plasticard as oblong boxes 10-mm high and 7-mm wide. Inside the box there are four cylinders made from plastic tubing or 2-mm

The centre chassis of the trailer is designed so that the wheels can be moved further inboard on narrow roads.

Folding hydraulic ramps are held in the raised position by chains.

The rear end of the trailer showing the folded ramps.

wide strip. Place these in position by referring to photographs.

The driveshaft extension is enclosed in a rectangular box 12-mm long. This is made from 0.5-mm strip, the box also requi-

ring two inspection covers in each corner.

Add the gearbox with its four driveshafts which should be enclosed in a small rectangular box 5-mm wide and 12-mm long and

reinforce the point where it makes a junction with the chassis with two pieces that form a 5-mm wide rectangle. Place the four shafts inside this box and construct a similar, identical box and fix both

Tool boxes and spare parts are carried on the trailer edges.

of them to the chassis. Although the rear trailer connectors come from a commercial kit, they need to have a additional flat plate with four nuts at the base. Again, the nuts come from a Verlinden kit. Hydraulic lines are formed from plastic strip and their semi-circular anchorage points are made using small round-end pliers of the kind used in electrical work. The sections of the trailer and triangular load supports are from 1.5-mm thick plasticard. Each should be 5-mm long and 5-mm wide.

Underside view of the cab showing the differential, wheel and spring arrangment.

MUDGUARDS

These are made from two thicknesses of 0.5-mm card, 7-mm wide and 18-mm in length. Add two 0.25-mm long strips 2-mm wide to make the three retaining nuts.

The four separate mudguards located on the rear of the cab section below the trailer arch are prepared using two sections of 0.25-mm plasticard bent to an angle. Forward of the rear quad set of wheels are the hydraulic and electrical connectors. These are made from different guages of copper wire. Locate these as indicated on photographs and the plans.

THE TRAILER

The trailer is built up using similar methods used to make the cab, so this section will concentrate only on some specific points to note. The two support beams are identical and made from 2-mm plasticard. The centre flatbed is cut out of 1.5-mm card, with the lower lateral reinforcement strips being made from 1-mm card. Two strips 1-mm thick and 5-mm wide - the same size as the flatbed reinforcements - are needed to complete this section. Card pieces 1.5-mm wide are shaped to attach the prime mover to the trailer, using a set square to ensure that a perfect 90 degree angle is obtained. When all the glue has dried, add further reinforcement to the inside of the flatbed with five 1.5-mm thick strips, each of which should be 5-mm wide.

Any remaining reinforcement should be carried out at this stage, again using 1.5-mm thick card.

Built for heavy duty load carrying, this transporter is able to lift all tracked vehicles used by the Spanish Army.

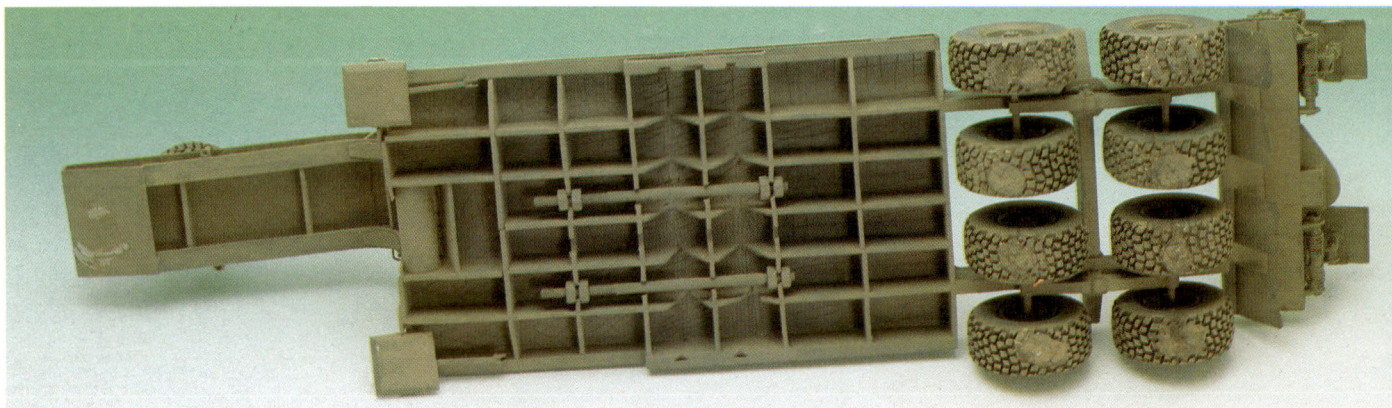

The size of the drive shaft alone indictates the immense lifting ability of the transporter

The differential bell housing and double leaf springs.

The underside of the trailer is protected by numerous grille sections which could be substituted by solid plastic rectangles.

The centre differential situated below the cab and trailer joint.

Trailing arms help distribute the load evenly throughout the trailer.

The trailer wheels are free rather than driven.

Refer to the plans to check the number of long and short reinforcement strips that are required. The two rear sections of the trailer are constructed and glued using the methods previously described.

Add a semi-circular support for the winch that retains the hawser used to assist in loading vehicles onto the trailer. The central flatbed and trailer joint are also covered with 0.5-mm plastic sheet.

The three sections of non-slip floor surfacing which on this model was made from photo-etch metal sheet, is glued on with cyanoacrylate.

Axle locking pins are made from 3-mm brass and 30-mm long round-section strip. Trim these to

Heavy duty springs retain the tail ramps

Fuel tanks and an electric winch with its wire hawser.

Heavy duty jacks are situated in the front and rear of the trailer.

fit each axle end, using a drop of cyanoacrylate adhesive and filler as necessary. Trim the hubcaps to fit each of the outside tyres snugly, adding a 13.5-mm diameter retaining plate on the inside of each wheel. A 3-mm hole in each axle retains the locking pins. Detailing of the trailer and rear ramps starts with constructing a support for the crane, necessitating cutting out a 1-mm thick piece of plasticard. This should be 4-mm wide by 7-mm long, formed to shape by referring to the plans. At the end of the semi-circle you will need to bore two 1.5-mm diameter holes to take the crane supports, each of which should consist of a 2-mm length of tubing. Curved lateral reinforcement sections 1-mm thick, 5-mm wide and 10-mm long, need to be located in the area where the transmission train links up to the trailer. The pulleys that guide the steel hawser have their own small axles, these also being made out of plastic tubing. At the base of the pulleys, the stee

Details at the rear of the trailer include a towing hook.

Hub detail differs on the prime mover and trailer wheels

Tie-down bars and wheel chocks are situated on the trailer link arm.

Building into a very impressive model in its own right, a transporter is also a good place to park a model tank!

Since World War II the world's armies have had tank transporters so there is a wide range for the modeller to chose from.

mounting plates are reproduced by putty and plastic discs.

TRAILER RESTRAINING JACKS

For the four jacks that restrain the vehicle during loading and unloading operations you need to cut eight 17-mm long plasticard sections each 0.5-mm wide. They will eventually form a box section when edge pieces from 0.5-mm thick card 2-mm wide are added. Make these pieces 18-mm long with a 45 degree cut at each corner. To these box sections are glued 5-mm squares from 1.5-mm card, each with a 2-mm diameter hole in the centre. Round section strips 35-mm long are then located in the holes.

Make the vehicle chocks from 1-mm plasticard referring again to the vehicle plans which detail these items. Each set of stops needs adjacent handgrips made from 0.75-mm copper wire.

The steel cable guides on the winches are all made from 1-mm plasticard.

Vehicle height adjusters should be made from 1.5-mm thick card.

Guide strips on the rear trailer require four identical pieces from 1.5-mm thick card. A 2-mm hole is drilled in the upper part of each piece. Locate inside a 2-mm diameter tube which should be 40-mm long. With all four pieces complete, add these to the trailer in the appropriate places.

All loading ramps, which should be 5-mm wide, are constructed from 1-mm card. At approximately the half way point a reinforcement is added, with a second one located to support the hinged section. Hinges can be either the long or short type.

Springs:

These are made from 0.8-mm copper wire rolled around a 2-mm drill handle to obtain the correct spiral effect.

Locking pins:

Make these from 2-mm diameter tubing, each of them being 18-mm long.

Exterior hinges:

Cut to size using 1-mm thick plastic rod.

Interior hinges:

For these cut plasticard sections 2-mm thick with the upper part rounded off with a file.

Finish the model off by glueing two supports to the ramps, as described, using two 1-mm plastic pieces each 8-mm in length. Round them off and drill a 2-mm hole to take the locking pin that prevents free movement across the floor.

Reference photos will show that this transporter carries its own crane on the right hand side of the trailer. The crane can be constructed from 0.5-mm card sections of plastic sheet. Three locating rings need to be made up from 0.8-mm copper wire. The spare wheel retainer is made with 0.5-mm card cut to an 8-mm wide, 20-mm long section.